FINANCIAL DECISION MAKING FOR SUCCESS

FINANCIAL DECISION MAKING FOR SUCCESS

ERIC HOOGSTRA, PHD, CFP®

Financial Decision Making for Success
Copyright © 2018 by Eric J. Hoogstra
All rights reserved.

Published in the United States by Credo House Publishers,
a division of Credo Communications, LLC, Grand Rapids, Michigan
credohousepublishers.com

ISBN: 978-1-625861-25-2

Cover and interior design by Frank Gutbrod
Editing by Michael A. Vander Klipp

Printed in the United States of America
First edition

Names and other details have been changed to protect the privacy of the individuals whose stories are told in this book.

CONTENTS

SESSION 1: INTRODUCTION 1
"Why Didn't I Know This Already?" 4
You Can Change Your Financial Future 6
Skills Necessary to Be Successful in Financial Management 8
Determining Your Financial Situation 10
A Successful Life 11

SESSION 2: GOALS, GOALS, AND MORE GOALS! 13
Setting Both Short- and Long-Term Goals 14
Defining Your Goals 15
Categories of Goals 16
Prioritizing Your Goals 24
Putting It All Together 25
Do All These Goals Really Need to Be Written? 26
The Next Step: Action! 27

SESSION 3: BUDGETING 29
Variable Expenses 30
First-Pass Budget 31
So Now What? 31
Keys to Effective Budgeting 32
Budgeting Systems 39
Defining Needs vs. Wants 42
Knowing Your Financial Condition in Six Easy Steps 43
Balancing Your Budget and Creating a Margin for Goals 54

Determining the Necessary Changes 56
Breaking Down Absolute vs. Non-Absolute Expenses 57
Ideas for Balancing Your Budget 58
The Problems with Debt 70
Shop Until We Drop? 71
Credit Cards 73
Buying Too Much House 76
Buying Instead of Renting 79
Is It Really Location, Location, Location? 80
Autos 80
The Lottery/Gambling Trap 86
Co-Signing for Someone Else 88
Making the Commitment to Change 89
Employee Benefits 90

SESSION 4: EFFECTIVE INVESTING 95

Understanding Investment Options 95
Understanding the Time Value of Money 107
Understanding Your Personal Risk Tolerance 110
Your First Investment 112
Your Second Investment 113
Considering New Investment Options 114
Separating Investment Vehicles from Investments 114
Active vs. Passive Investing 115
Technical Analysis and Market Timing 117
Matching Investments with Available Time 119
What About Risk? 120
Asset Allocation 122
Selecting Appropriate Securities 123
Setting Up Your Brokerage Account 125
Get-Rich-Quick Schemes 132
How Can We Teach Children? 133
Understanding Financial Designations 137

SESSION 5: INSURANCE, TAXATION, RETIREMENT, AND ESTATE PLANNING   139

Insurance   139
Taxation   144
Retirement   146
Estate Planning   158

WORKSHEETS   167

Worksheet 1 *Debt Listing Worksheet*   167
Worksheet 2 *Balance Sheet*   169
Worksheet 3 *A Successful Life*   171
Worksheet 4 *Long-Term Goals*   173
Worksheet 5 *5-Year Prioritized Goals*   175
Worksheet 6 *Goal Development Form*   177
Worksheet 7 *Variable Expenses*   179
Worksheet 8 *First-Pass Budget*   181
Worksheet 9 *Suggested Budget Spending Ranges*   183
Worksheet 10 *Budget Comparison to Ranges*   185
Worksheet 11 *Absolutes/Non-Absolutes*   187
Worksheet 12 *Goal Costs*   189
Worksheet 13 *Debt Snowball*   191
Worksheet 14 *Ideas for Balancing the Budget*   193
Worksheet 15 *Revised Final Budget*   195
Worksheet 16 *Employer Benefits Checklist*   197
Worksheet 17 *Savings Plan*   199
Worksheet 18 *Insurance Needs*   201
Worksheet 19 *Estate Planning Document*   203

SESSION 1

INTRODUCTION

If someone were to ask you today about your current financial situation, what would you say? If you're a typical American, you might reply in one or more of the following ways:

- You are frustrated that you are working harder and harder yet getting further and further behind with your bills and payments.
- Your growing credit card or student loan debt gives you a sense of hopelessness.
- Your home equity loan or second mortgage application has been turned down by yet another bank.
- You are meeting your current payments but are worried about some of the longer-term issues of college planning for the children or the costs of retirement for yourself.
- You think you are on the right track financially, but you want to be sure.
- You are continually receiving financial statements from your company's 401(k), but you have no idea what they mean or which investment options you should choose.
- You are looking for some overall direction with regard to your finances.

- You are looking to make changes with regard to your finances that are more in line with your specific situations and goals.

Finally, you are a college student who has not been provided an example of how to make good financial decisions throughout your life and are uncertain how to handle your finances when you get out of college. Whatever your circumstances, you are about to embark on a course that will help you plan, execute, and hopefully change your financial future.

While many of you do not have current financial issues, when you exit college and get into the real world it will be easy to get into financial problems and to struggle financially. Most people do! When this happens, you have to understand four realities upfront. First, you are not the only one who will experience such problems. If you talk to your friends and acquaintances, you will find many others facing similar concerns.

Second, financial problems do not have to be a normal part of life. If you so desire, you can greatly change your direction and situation. If you are one of those people who wants to take action, this book has been written for you!

Third, this book/course is designed to help you assess your current financial situation and guide you in making lifelong changes to become more financially secure and to meet the goals you have set for yourself.

Finally, this book was written to help you manage your finances so you can be a responsible manager of all your financial resources. Regardless of your current situation, or the depth of your financial problems, this book/course will enable you to effectively manage your resources better from here on out. Finance should not be a stressful process! The only way you will fail is if you fail to plan!

Each of our financial stories and situations is unique, and each personal financial situation will require a different set of solutions to solve those issues. As you continue through this course and book, you will find that I will not provide a one-size-fits-all approach. Instead, I will give you the tools for exploring various options and allow you to develop your own individual plan.

In addition, this book is designed not only to help you assess your current financial situation but to give you the tools you need to move much more quickly toward the goals you create for yourselves and to achieve financial freedom (I would define this as freedom from the worry of debt or financial problems). You have the ability to move toward your goals if you take responsible and purposeful actions. As you move closer to this goal each day, you will substantially reduce the stresses and financial pressures that plague your life and will greatly increase your peace and contentment. In fact, increased contentment may be even more beneficial than reduced stress.

While this is our goal, for most Americans it doesn't always work that way. A number of researchers who study trends in personal finance in America have come up with some striking findings:

- Almost half of all Americans spend more per year than they earn.
- Money management is the #1 source of marital conflict today. In fact, 90 percent of divorces today point to financial issues as one of the primary causes.
- The average American carries a credit card balance of more than $10,000 (this figure tends to go up by about $1,000 per year, and this normally happens around Christmastime).
- More than $800 billion is owed on credit cards today.
- Money mismanagement, as well as not having a budget, causes the average American to use an ATM machine to obtain cash about every other day.

- More money is spent today on gambling than on groceries. This trap has caused many of us to base our financial futures on luck or chance.
- Personal bankruptcy rates have grown exponentially in recent years.
- The number of home foreclosures has jumped dramatically. While this increase in the number of foreclosures alone may not be a concern, a number of people are renting homes from landlords who face possible foreclosure, which will cause renters to lose their homes in the process.

As you consider these findings, it is important to keep in mind that many Americans are probably in worse financial shape than you are.

Many individuals and families today face severe financial difficulties, even if most do not talk about it. This creates a sense of hopelessness for those who incorrectly believe they are the only ones in financial distress. This belief is flat wrong!

When you openly discuss your finances with others, you will find that many have the same problems you do or worse. By sharing and working together, you can support and hold each other accountable as you seek to change your financial future.

"Why Didn't I Know This Already?"

Many individuals feel that the financial condition they are in is the result of the lack of certain financial skills. One question often asked of me is "Why didn't I know this already?" or "Why was I never taught this in school?" To be honest, these are excellent questions to which I don't have good answers.

In Michigan, school districts require each student to take advanced math courses as part of the required curriculum.

However, Michigan still does not require students to take any personal finance courses or even teach students how to balance a checkbook. In fact, one can earn a PhD from a reputable university without learning basic personal financial management skills or how to balance a checkbook. That is really sad!

So where do people learn how to manage their finances today? Unfortunately, most of this training is the responsibility of parents and society. However, most parents also missed much of this training and therefore may not be a good source of such information.

> ### PRACTICAL EXAMPLE
> *Many researchers are watching the changing behavior of the Baby Boomer generation. These individuals represent almost one-third of America's adult population. Historically, Baby Boomers have been responsible for the development and growth of many businesses (including McDonald's), but as they grow older their spending patterns are changing. These changes in spending patterns have caused many businesses to rethink their business models. In addition, many of these Boomers have not prepared for and saved enough for retirement. As the balances of Social Security go down, it will be interesting to watch how this group readjusts their lifestyles within the realities retirement may provide for them.*

Society's guidance, based upon its emphasis on constant consumption, constant advertising, and multiple credit card offers, also may not be an acceptable source of proper information concerning personal finance.

You Can Change Your Financial Future

At this point you may be asking yourself *Can I really change my finances and my financial future?* Thankfully, this frequently asked question can be answered with a resounding Yes! At this point you may see problems and despair. Within the next four sessions, however, I want to instill in you a new vision of confidence, hope, and destiny.

> ### PRACTICAL EXAMPLE
> *Steve and Bethany have seven children. Steve was earning a salary of $25,000 per year, and Bethany was a stay-at-home mom. Over the years they accumulated more than $40,000 in credit card debt. Through learning and studying, commitment, and changes in their lifestyle, they eliminated all of their debt within five years. Accomplishing so much in such a relatively brief period of time is not uncommon when it becomes one of your focus areas.*

I often compare personal finance with personal weight loss. You just need to do the math. If you are eating 3,000 calories per day, which is about 500 calories per day more than you are expending, you will gain one pound every seven days. If you cut your daily calorie intake by 500 calories or 16.7 percent, you will break even. If you want to lose weight, you need to eat fewer than 2,500 calories or exercise more to expend more calories. If you reduce your dietary intake by another 500 calories, a total reduction of one-third of your previous intake, it will take seven days to lose one pound. Keep it up for six months and you'll lose twenty-six pounds.

As with weight loss, our personal finances may require us to make cuts in our spending (eating less) or to take on additional jobs to earn more (exercise).

As with weight loss, there is no "magic pill" or secret solution to get our finances back on track. The last thing we want to do is bounce from one diet (budgeting system) to another. Instead, we need to change our behavior. There is no secret formula to make all of your financial problems go away. Unfortunately, I cannot wave a magic wand and cause your financial problems to disappear. Changing your financial situation will take time, effort, and dedication on your part. Many people take several years to dramatically change their financial condition. But my clients always say they would do it again, thanks to the many benefits they now enjoy.

> **PRACTICAL EXAMPLE**
>
> *Ryan and Beth currently have $5,000 in credit card debt. They have two options for paying this debt: (1) pay a minimal amount of $75 per month, or (2) cut back on some of their expenses and pay $150 each month toward this debt. If they make the minimum payments, it will take 283 months to pay off this debt at a total cost of $21,225. If Ryan and Beth pay $150 per month, however, they can eliminate this debt in 45.5 months at a total cost of only $6,825. Overall, option 2 would save $14,400 and give them the joys of financial freedom almost 20 years faster than option 1.*

> ### PRACTICAL EXAMPLE
>
> *Ben and Myra want to take a vacation and have determined that they could put aside $50 per month for the $3,000 cruise of their dreams. If they decide to take the trip now (they saw the credit card advertisements, after all, and discovered they deserve one), it will take them 146 months (more than 12 years at 18 percent) to pay for that wonderful but brief vacation. If they save up, however, Ben and Myra will be able to go on a fully paid cruise in only 48 months (4 years) if they earn 10 percent on their saved money. That's a difference of more than 8 years, time enough to save for two more $3,000 luxury cruises. Their motto: Save now to have more fun later!*

Individuals and couples I have worked with in the past made significant progress toward their financial goals within a few years and eventually even became debt free if they were willing to make the necessary lifestyle adjustments. Therefore, regardless of your current situation, I can assure you that there is hope for your future! I can further assure you that the time you spend working though this seven-day money makeover will be both life-changing and well worth the effort!

Skills Necessary to Be Successful in Financial Management

Many individuals falsely believe that they are "numerically challenged" or do not have the necessary mathematical or financial skills to balance their checkbook or invest for the future effectively. As a result, they create needless chaos for themselves and others.

> **PRACTICAL EXAMPLE**
>
> *Some people maintain three or four checking accounts. Each month they use one of them to deposit their paychecks and write their checks. As they do not understand how to balance their checking accounts, after the end of the month they begin using another account. They rotate through these accounts. When it comes time to use an account again, they call the bank and enter the bank's balance as the starting balance. Talk about a juggling act!*

In reality, managing your financial resources is a relatively simple process. It certainly does not require using any high-level mathematics. You need only to have the basic skills for addition, subtraction, multiplication, and division.

More important than numerical skills, you must be prudent in managing the resources provided to you. All it takes is an honest willingness to make some behavioral changes so you don't spend more than you make.

If we need relatively few skills to manage our finances properly, why do so many people have financial issues and problems? One of the reasons is the "I want it now" attitude we all possess, thanks to years of marketing and advertising that have conditioned us to get it now and pay later.

Thankfully, over the next two weeks you can reverse your thinking, make positive changes in your life, and enjoy the satisfaction that comes from making good financial decisions.

In the course Introduction I asked you a simple question: How do you perceive your current financial condition? Many individuals believe their financial situation is bad but don't understand the true magnitude of their problems. This misperception causes them to incorrectly believe they can manage things, when in reality they are on a collision course with financial disaster.

Just being able to pay all of your current bills on time is not necessarily a sign of financial stability. You may still be missing some longer-term needs and goals, such as saving for retirement or for your children's education.

Then again, consistently being unable to pay your bills on time usually indicates significant problems with your finances. The constant pressure of having to select which bills to pay this week or month causes stress, both in our personal lives and within our relationships, including our relationships with those we love the most. Also, by focusing on these short-term problems we often ignore our higher priorities, frequently miss the larger picture of life, and all too often neglect our own longer-term goals. In short, having financial problems causes undue stress and negatively affects relationships.

This chapter was designed to guide you through a series of simple but important steps. These steps will allow you (and your spouse or partner if you have one) to assess your current financial situation, determine what a successful life looks like for you, develop both short- and long-term goals, review the strategies and barriers you have in achieving these goals, and create the first pass on your budget.

Determining Your Financial Situation

The first step in today's session is to determine where you are at financially. This will involve three steps. First, using Worksheet 1 you will list all of your debts. This may include credit card balances, auto loans, and student loan debt you have accumulated. While this may be a depressing process, it is an important first step. On this worksheet you will list not only the amounts but also who they are owed to and the interest rate on each. Second, we will use this information in creating a personal balance sheet. What you may find after this process is that your overall net worth at this point in your life is negative. While this is definitely not desired, at this point it may be a reality for you. Once you have these two items completed, a third may be to ask for a credit report for you to review. There are several firms (including Experian, Equifax, Transunion, and CreditKarma) that offer you a free credit report each year. It is important that you request this periodically throughout your life to make sure it is accurate. If there are any issues with items on this report, these organizations also provide instructions on how to report them.

A Successful Life

Once we have determined our current financial status, we can look at what defines success for us. Again, each of us will define success differently. While we may think we know what it takes to be a successful person today, this definition may change as we move through life. For example, for many years I measured success by titles, achievements, and life toys. As I got older I became much more interested in my relationships and personal legacy. Defining what a successful life looks like for you will determine the course you want for your life. I would like to offer you one word of caution at this point in the process. If you state that money is your measure of success, you will always find that there is someone who has more than you have, and most likely you will never be content with what you have (even if you make millions each year). Take some time using Worksheet 3 to script what a successful life would look like for you. You may find it easier to do this assignment by projecting yourself into the future and then looking back on your life to determine what has been truly important to you.

SESSION 2

GOALS, GOALS, AND MORE GOALS!

Setting life goals will help you determine both how your funds need to be invested and the resources you'll need to achieve these goals. Each New Year millions of Americans make resolutions to lose weight, become more physically fit, or spend less money. While some of these individuals succeed in their goals, the majority do not last beyond the first week. Why is this? Why can't we achieve the goals we set for ourselves? I believe that one of the main reasons for this is that we have no compelling reason to do so. Achieving these goals would provide no specific benefit to us—either materially or personally. The bottom line is that we just don't have a good enough "why" these goals are important for us to achieve. In addition, goals should be used to move us from the person we are to the person we are striving to become. Yet without your taking the time to determine what type of person we would like to become, setting goals will just involve a task list to be resurrected again next year.

When developing our goals, we need to take a serious look at who we are, the direction we want to go, and what we want to become during our lives. Such goals instill passion and motivate us to actually accomplish them.

In this section you will be developing and prioritizing your goals and then looking to see, based on your projected resources, which ones you will be able to accomplish. As you develop your high priority goals, it will be important to spell out in detail the first steps you will need to take to attain them.

Most of you will have more goals than you have the resources to accomplish. Does that mean you should remove certain goals from your list? Definitely not! As you move through life some of your goals may change, and you may gain additional resources that could fund either new or existing goals.

Setting Both Short- and Long-Term Goals

As you begin developing your goals, think in both the short and the long term. Although society continually pushes us toward short-term thinking, we must continually be aware of the longer-term needs that require our financial resources.

I recently saw an advertisement for a car I would like to have. When I became aware of the monthly cost of the vehicle, my first response was that I could afford it. Although I could afford it, if I purchased this vehicle I would be thinking in the short term only. By purchasing the vehicle today, I may not have the financial resources I might need to fund longer-term goals for myself and my family.

> **TRANSFORMATIONAL TIP**
>
> *We cannot continue to spend for today and not consider the future.*

How do we prevent short-term thinking? By defining both short- and long-term life goals! Take the time to do this. It will make a significant difference in your future!

Defining Your Goals

If you were just diagnosed with a terminal illness and were given only one year to live, how would you want to live out that year? What experiences would you like to have, and how would you treat your relationships with others? Since most of us do not know the number of days in our future, should we not live every day as though it were our last?

Barring a situation like that in the previous paragraph, at this point in your journey you need to develop a complete list of all the goals you would like to achieve over the next 10 years. These goals include specific aspirations for your family, educational ideals, travel plans, significant acquisitions you would like to make, etc.

I highly encourage you (along with your spouse or partner) to take some time, maybe even to get away for a period of time, to jointly develop your household goals. If you are single, you may want to work with a friend or accountability partner. As you work through this process, it is important to make these goals as specific as possible. For example, here are two goals:

- I would like to be debt-free.
- I will be debt-free by December 31, 20XX.

Which goal inspires you more? The first doesn't have a specific deadline and no confident assurance that you will successfully complete it. Sure, I "would like" to have a number of good things, but unless I create a goal as though I expect to achieve it ("I will") and set a time frame within which to reach it, there is little chance I will succeed.

In addition, as you develop your goals it is important to remember that at this stage in the process no goal is out of the question or too impossible to achieve. Just use the worksheet to keep listing goals until you feel as though you have developed a comprehensive list. I would not be surprised if, as you start listing your goals in each of these areas, you may develop a list of 100, 200, or even more possible goals you'd like to achieve over the remainder your life.

Categories of Goals

As you begin to develop your goals, it is important to begin to categorize them to ensure that they support a balanced life. In this course we will define goals in five specific areas: family, financial, professional or career, personal, and physical.

Don't view goal setting as just another task to check off on a list. Rather, allow these goals to inspire you to consider who you want to become as a person. Keep all areas of your life in mind. We've all heard accounts of business leaders who poured all of their energy and resources into their work, only to experience negative (and oftentimes disastrous) consequences with their spouse and children. Focusing on only one area, such as a career, will only cause you to become frustrated and experience difficulties in other areas of your life.

Family Goals

According to Patrick Morley, author of *Man in the Mirror*, no amount of success we may experience at work will ever compensate for failure at home. One of our primary responsibilities is to others within our family: as a husband, a wife, a partner, a child, a parent. All family members carry responsibilities toward each other. A great many people today cite financial reasons for failing relationships. I believe, however, that financial problems are just one of the surface issues and that often other relationship issues are at stake. More often than not, financial problems are just a cover-up for problems in other areas.

Although financial issues are an important part of family life, taking the necessary time to cultivate relationships is also vital. If you were to look back 25 years from now, what would determine whether you were a successful spouse, partner, or parent?

Although most of you do not have children at this point in your life, someday I hope you will. I am reminded that children spell love as T-I-M-E! Time spent with our children is a responsibility— and an invaluable investment. The pressures of the world often reduce time spent with our children to a minimum. Many parents today work such long hours that they don't have sufficient time to spend with their children. I often wonder why we needed to move from the standard of a one-parent income to that of a two-parent income in less than one generation. In many families both spouses are pursuing individual career goals, but it is often the case that both are working just to purchase more "toys" or the "stuff" to appear more successful.

Children have become of secondary importance at a time when it is more critical than ever for parents to prepare their children for life and to raise them up. I often see parents spend hours with their kids on sports, and their children can recite many statistics of various sports teams and players. I would recommend that you encourage your children and appreciate their achievements regardless of how small they are; love them unconditionally regardless of what they do.

For many of you, the realities of divorce in your family or the sadness of a poor childhood experience may be weighing quite heavily on your heart at this point. You cannot change what has happened in the past, but you need to remember that you are still alive. You still have time to work on your relationships and bring about peace and possible reconciliation.

As you review your family relationships, you may want to set specific goals for spending the time to make family relationships one of your highest priorities. I firmly believe that positive results will follow! As you list the goals that will strengthen your family life, also list what those goals will do for you if achieved.

Financial Goals

Of course, setting financial goals is essential. Some of the financial goals you may want to consider are to reduce or eliminate your debt, to increase your personal savings, to save for a child's education, or to save for retirement. Although these may be included with your other personal goals, including them under this category will allow you to focus your financial resources on achieving them.

Professional Goals

It is important to bear in mind that we do not know what the future will hold for us. I am sure that many of you at one time hoped for a change in career or a job promotion and were disappointed by not receiving it. After a period of time, another opportunity opened up that was significantly better than the previous one, and you realize that, if you'd had your way and taken the first position, you would have been disappointed.

Everyone desires to make a difference and to achieve something significant. That said, are you excited about waking up in the morning and going to work? If the statistics are reliable, depending on which statistic you read, about 60 to 80 percent of you do not like your job. According to one survey 90 percent of individuals lead a defeated life, and over 80 percent of the population goes to work in a job they hate. That is sad for us Americans who live in the land of opportunity! The question I would ask those of you who do not like your job (now or in the future) is this: What are you doing to move yourself toward a position in which you can be excited about getting up in the morning, passionate about the work you will do that day?

One of the principles I have always lived by is that life is too short to have a job you hate, regardless of how much money it pays. One of my greatest personal accomplishments is that I have a job that I love and that fits my personality perfectly. This was not always the case. For a long time I looked primarily at the money I could make in a job, not about getting a job I loved to get up every day and do.

Changing my focus from how much money I made to following my vocational passion did not happen overnight; it was a process I worked on for a number of years. Most Americans want instant results, and a longer-term process of moving toward a career they could enjoy seems like too much work. I can assure you, however, that the benefits in my case have been significant.

Some of the goals we will focus on in this section are the industry we would like to work in, the company we would like to work for, the position level we are trying to achieve, and the pay we would like to obtain. If you are in sales, your goals may include the level of sales you wish to achieve each year and even the possibility of owning your own business.

In my case, I knew I wanted to become a teacher. To do that I needed to go on for additional training, including the attainment of a PhD, which took a number of years to complete. For some of you it may be important to develop a network of people who can begin to work with you and will help you in the future.

For example, if you would like to become a human resources director, you may want to develop a resource network that requires you to become a member of a society of human resources professionals, or a member of a CEO organization that would be full of people who might potentially hire you in the future.

Some of you may not know what career path to take, or what type of work you would enjoy doing. Thankfully, there are a number of instruments available through job training services, high school and college vocational counselors, and various internet sites that can help you with this decision. One of the exceptional tests is the Campbell Interest and Skill Inventory (CISS), which is available from a number of sources, including the internet.

Some individuals have a goal of owning their own business. In fact, over the past decade almost all of the growth in employment has come from smaller businesses. One area you could explore is turning some of your activities or hobbies into a money-making venture.

I firmly believe that everyone should have "multiple streams of income" that can provide additional current income and serve as a buffer in case of job loss. These additional sources of income can lessen the blows of economic changes and reduce the negative effects of globalization that many will experience. If we take a few moments we can all list a few things we are already doing that we could turn into a business venture.

With the benefits of technology, anyone can open a business from his bedroom or garage and make himself appear to be as large as General Electric. If you have an interest in this area, I hope you continue to explore the benefits this could bring to you.

Your career is one of the most important aspects of providing personal significance in your life. Are you satisfied with how your career is progressing? If you are, what might make your life even better? If not, what actions can you take in order to begin the process of moving toward your life's plan?

Are you enjoying your work? If not, what are you doing to move toward a career in which you can use your specific talents in service to others?

Personal Goals

Your goals in this section encompass your relationships with others, your emotional state, and the process of self-improvement. I am reminded of the song that states that if you want to change the world, you must begin with yourself. There are those of us who may believe we are close to perfect. However, those who know us best not only know our limitations but can also give us many suggestions for improvement. This feedback may at times be a painful reminder of how imperfect we are, but it will humble us as we try to improve.

Our friends are an important aspect of our personal relationships. They share our joys and comfort us during our times of grief. They congratulate us when we succeed and help us get back up when we fall down.

How would you answer the following question: How many true friends do you have? Sort through the list of your many acquaintances and focus on those who are most significant to you. Take the necessary time to develop your relationships with those you consider to be your true friends.

Another question: What specific actions have you taken in the last 30 days to further develop these true friendships? Perhaps you realize that many times you have taken these important relationships for granted. List a few goals for developing people skills that will improve your relationships with others.

In times of increasing globalization, individuals who stay ahead of others on the knowledge curve seem to always have an occupation. Unfortunately, spending an increasingly significant amount of time on unproductive activities, such as watching television, doesn't move anyone ahead in knowledge.

I believe that increasing numbers of people know more about what is happening on the popular TV shows than they do about the changes going on within their career or the direction of the general economy. For some of you, the need for an increase in knowledge may require you to attend additional classes in school. For everyone else, visiting the library or doing other research will help you upgrade your occupational skills.

Today, in the informational and digital age, just keeping abreast of the current developments will require increasing amounts of time and effort. College students in their junior and senior years may be studying facts that had not yet been discovered when they were freshman.

Ask yourself two questions as you develop goals in this area. First, what are you doing to make sure you are upgrading your knowledge and skill set within your field of work? Second, what could you be doing to significantly increase your knowledge?

For some of you, this may be as simple as turning off the television and picking up a book to read. For others who are in a position that may be outsourced within the next few years, it may mean setting goals toward transitioning to a new career. For still others it may mean learning an additional language in order to remain competitive or moving to another country in order to provide a living for yourself and your family. I am sure that as you develop goals within this section you will find many opportunities to allow you to succeed in the future.

Physical Goals

Okay, I know what you are saying: I am 20 years old, and I look and feel great, so why should I care about this? Well, I have news for you: the health decisions you make today will have an effect on you not only today but for many years in the future. In my case, not caring about what I ate or drank when I was your age has taken its toll on my body, and the lack of proper decisions in this area when I was in my 20s and 30s are affecting me today. To achieve the many goals we have developed thus far, we need to be in good physical shape. The rat race of daily existence has resulted in too many of us settling for fast food as we drive from appointment to appointment or drinking on the weekends just to "get away" from life for a few hours.

Physical activity for many of us has become limited to keyboarding, playing video games, or walking back and forth to the parking lot at work. Many of us may have health club memberships but rarely use them because we are unable to get there because of our work schedules and time pressures. These memberships just become a wasted monthly expense. While this is not the case for all, it has become the norm for many Americans.

All of this abuse of our bodies has taken a toll, and for many of us obesity and its related diseases are becoming more and more common. If you take the time to talk to someone who schedules time each week for physical activity, he will describe the benefits of this activity and tell you how this has made him more productive in other areas of his life.

As you set goals for your physical health, consider what type of person you would like to become as a result of a particular habit or activity. What would you like to achieve, and how would this benefit you personally? Becoming physically fit may allow you to live longer and to spend more time with your spouse, children, and even your grandchildren! You may not see the benefit of exercise now, but taking a longer view will cause you to give physical activity a higher priority.

So, what type of physical goals should you set for yourself? That question depends on where you are physically and what form of physical fitness you believe you need in order to move forward. Based on your age, it may not be reasonable to expect that you will once again be able to achieve "six-pack" abs or a sculpted body.

It may be more reasonable to set a goal of getting a proper number of hours of rest each night or taking the stairs at work instead of the elevators. It may also be reasonable to begin a smoking cessation plan and/or an exercise routine and to resist junk food and sugary drinks between meals. For some, having a goal of losing an additional 20 pounds may be a significant undertaking. For others this may be a very reasonable and quickly achievable goal.

Finally, it is important to remember that before you act on any of your physical goals you are wise to seek the advice of your doctor. She will help you focus on the goals that will provide the greatest benefits and advise you concerning additional action steps required to achieve greater success in this area. What are your goals for physical well-being?

Prioritizing Your Goals

Now it's time to prioritize your goals. Prioritize them on the basis of the time and resources they will require. Unfortunately, you do not have unlimited time or financial resources to apply to your goals. Select goals that require your immediate focus and leave others for the future, should you gain additional resources.

It is important to remember that you can achieve any goal you want. However, you will most likely not be able to achieve all of your goals. Does this mean we need to remove some of our goals from our list? No, but be selective and focus your energy and resources on the ones that are most important to you.

You may determine that you have sufficient financial resources to achieve only the top three goals on your list. Although your children's education may be important to you, it may be number eight on the list. If it is not realistic to be able to achieve the goal of funding your children's education, you may need to inform them early on so they can focus on sports or getting good grades to increase their chance at getting scholarships. Or they may choose to take a job during high school to begin saving toward the cost of college. This may sound rather harsh, but it is part of prioritization. You can achieve any goal you set your mind to, but it's unlikely you can achieve them all.

As you prioritize your goals, don't just consider your needs and desires. Be sure to include all of the individuals affected by the process. Other goals, such as new living room furniture, may be more important to your wife or your social circle than the new bass boat that you want.

Once you have completed this step it may be helpful to re-list your goals in order of priority. The prioritization of your goals is a key step in the financial planning process—don't skimp on it!

Putting It All Together

So, how are we going to put this all together? How are we going to process the goals we have identified? Our first step is to list all the goals we would like to achieve over the next 10 years. Our aim at this point is listing them quantitatively (the more the better) rather than qualitatively (Can I really achieve this?). Our goal is to create 150 of them in just 30 minutes or less. While this may seem a difficult task at this point, only 30 individual goals in each of the areas we have previously listed would add up to 150 goals. Using Worksheet 4, list the goals you have for your life over the next 10 years.

Once we have the master list, we are going to prioritize it to determine which are most important for us to achieve now. For example, for most of you attaining your college degree is one of the most important goals you now have, and many of your other goals depend on your attaining this one. Therefore, this will likely be one of your most important goals. Finding a job after college may come in as a close second. If these are among your goals, make sure you assign them a high priority. Using Worksheet 5, list the top 20 goals you have right now. I have no doubt all of you are highly capable in mathematics, and if you do the math you will note that you should be able to accomplish all of your 150 goals over the next 37½ years—which will roughly coincide with your working career. After that you can set another 150 goals for your retirement years.

After determining your five-year goals, it is always good to list the ones that are most important to you right now. Studies have shown that most people can manage a maximum of only five things at one time. Worksheet 6 allows you to list these five key goals. It also provides an area where you can list the projected timetable, potential obstacles to be overcome, and next action steps for achievement.

Do All These Goals Really Need to Be Written?

I know that many of you are asking, Now that I have these goals in my head and know what I want to do in life, do I really need to take the time to list them on paper? The short answer is yes! In a number of studies over the years the effectiveness of having written goals has been consistently demonstrated. For example, in one study of recent graduates from an Ivy League University, the graduating class was asked how many of them had written out their goals. The authors of the study found that 10 percent had taken the time to do this. When, after a period of 20 years, the authors went back and studied these students, they found that the 10 percent who had written out their goals had accomplished more than the other 90 percent combined. Our goals need to be written and reviewed on a regular basis in order to be effective and achievable. It is important to remember that just the process of writing out our goals moves us closer to their achievement. I think you will find it amazing how fast you will achieve goals that you had thought would take years.

The Next Step: Action!

After you have prioritized your goals, it is time to make them a reality. Worksheet 14 provides assistance with implementing some of your high priority goals. You can list your high priority goals on this worksheet and identify any potential obstacles that might prevent you from achieving them.

This worksheet also allows you to list potential individuals who might hold you accountable as you work through this process and ensure that you stay on track. You can also specify the action steps you would need to take in order to make each goal a reality, and the time allowed for completing it.

For example, maybe one of your goals is going back for additional college education to prepare you for a new career. You can list the goal as "graduate with a bachelor's degree by 20XX." Some action steps you would need to take would be to investigate possible schools and complete an application. This may sound almost silly, but without taking the action of looking and applying, you will never achieve the educational goal you have set.

Motivational speaker Anthony Robbins states that the clearer your goals are, the more powerful they will be, and the higher the level of success you will have in achieving them.

SESSION 3

BUDGETING

"Too many people spend money they haven't earned to buy things they don't want to impress people they don't like."

—WILL ROGERS

In this session we will address several key problems that can derail the best of financial plans. Although many things can cause financial problems, a few crucial issues usually cause the greatest difficulties. We'll review each of these potential problem areas and offer practical solutions. These solutions will allow you to continue to progress toward your goal of financial freedom. So don't skip a single page! In this session you will also begin by determining your periodic variable expenses, your household income, and your reoccurring monthly expenses. After you have identified these amounts, you will determine your current level of assets and debts and your personal net worth. These steps are some of the most important you will take and therefore will take a bit more time than future steps. It is important that you work through this session's exercises accurately, honestly, and openly.

Watch out for needless disappointment or frustration as you work through these first steps. No matter how hard you try you cannot change the past, and it's a waste of time to assign blame.

Instead, you need to make a commitment to move forward toward a better, more rewarding future.

For most Americans, the completion of this session's steps will be sobering since many individuals and couples spend more than they make. In addition, the average person's credit card balance tops $9,000. That said, don't forget that you are not alone; many of your friends and neighbors are in the same position.

When you look at your neighbors and wonder *How can they afford that?* the truth is most likely that they can't. There will be a day of reckoning for them, too. You may have tried to "keep up with the Joneses" and found out firsthand that this path leads to financial despair.

So, as you walk through these first few steps, be encouraged that this is the beginning of a journey that will ultimately lead to complete and total financial freedom. What a joy that will be. Ready? Let's begin this process together!

The next stage in this session is to determine where your spending pattern is going and how much margin you have in your spending to achieve the goals you set in the previous section. At this point you may not have at your fingertips all the figures you need or know what you are/will be spending; mastering this is a process you can improve on over time and can use in every stage of your life.

Variable Expenses

What often makes the budgeting process difficult is that expenses are not always equal each month and that particular expenses may occur at only certain times each year. For example, the average American spends over $1,200 for Christmas presents. However, this expense occurs only in December of each year. The average American believes they will be able to pay this off in January; however, because of the lack of margin in their budget or other unexpected expenses, this amount goes on their credit cards, and the average credit card carrying balance grows by $1,200 per year in many households. Worksheet 7 suggests some of these variable areas to reflect on and list. Again, your figures may not be accurate at this point.

First-Pass Budget

The first part of the budgeting process is completing a first-pass budget. A worksheet to help us with this is located in the back of this book. After this first pass, we will either use what we are currently spending or what we project to spend in the future. While these figures may not be entirely accurate at this point, they will give you a point of reference with which to begin the process. You will start by entering either your current or your projected income and then what you are paying or expecting to pay for each of the categories listed. One of the issues you may find at this point is that when you list your projected expenses you may underestimate what you really will be spending. For example, property taxes alone will run $150–$200 per month for an average home. Cable, internet, and cell phone charges can easily add up to over $200 per month. Resist the temptation to list what you would like the amounts to be; be realistic, as the more accurate your projections are the better the outcome will be.

So Now What?

At the conclusion of this session you may be either excited or depressed. Many of you may have a significant margin (available discretionary income) in your budget. If this is the case, I would like you to ask yourself *If this is true, where is all of this money?* Most cannot adequately answer this question, which means that they are spending it but don't know where it's going. Some of you may be overspending your income and know that to fix the situation you will need to make significant changes. If your budget is balanced at this point, more changes may still be necessary to achieve the longer-term goals you have listed in the goal section.

Keys to Effective Budgeting

To ensure that you stay on track and don't revert back to old patterns of spending, it's time to finalize your household budget. With the possible exception of Bill Gates or Warren Buffett, everyone needs a budget.

Over the years I have seen many budgeting systems. Some are incredibly simplistic, while others are highly complicated. Before we talk about the mechanical aspects of budgeting, though, we should take time to review what I consider my top seven essential keys for effective budgeting.

Key 1: Find Something That Works for You and Stick with It!

The form your budget takes is not critical as long as it provides you with pertinent information to make effective financial decisions. Regardless of which budgeting system you choose, it will need to be personalized in order to meet your individual requirements.

My particular method of recording my monthly transactions and entering them into my budget may or may not work for you. My system works for me, but it is a result of many years of trial and error. For years now I have used Quicken, along with software on my cell phone that interfaces with this system. As I make expenditures, I enter this information into my cell phone, and it is uploaded to my Quicken software every time I sync the phone with my computer. In addition, all of my credit card transactions are automatically downloaded and matched with the information uploaded from my phone.

Most readers will probably say that my system sounds too high tech or complex. You need to find an effective system that works for you.

Often when an individual or couple starts using a system they run into problems and stop using it. That's the wrong course of action! If you are using a system that does not work for you, you should identify the specific factors causing problems and change them. Only if that doesn't work should you start looking for another system.

Key 2: Keep Your Budget Simple

Budgeting should not be complicated. Your system should have only enough categories to direct your spending and to track items you'll need to report later on when you do your taxes. Furthermore, your system should require no more than 20 to 30 minutes of your time per week. If your current budgeting system takes more than an hour of your time per week, you may want to look for ways to modify and streamline it.

> **PRACTICAL EXAMPLE**
>
> *At one of my budgeting seminars a person presented his intriguing budgeting system. It consisted of a single piece of paper the size of a business card. Each day this individual would write down his income and expenses for the day. He knew that if his income each day was more than his expenses he would not get into financial trouble. While I do not endorse any one single budgeting system, I believe that many of them will work quite well if they are used consistently. Furthermore, regardless of which system you select you'll need to personalize it based on your particular circumstances and needs.*

Key 3: Work on Your Budget Together

It is important that you develop your budget with a partner for two reasons: training and accountability. Formulating and maintaining your budget with someone else creates a valuable form of accountability.

If you are a single person, I encourage you to find a good friend who can help you set up your new budget and serve as your accountability partner.

If you're married, I trust that you're already working with your spouse on each of these exercises. Your spouse's involvement is essential!

Each time I purchase something, I know that my wife will be looking at that expenditure at the end of the month with me and will have something to say if my spending is out of line. Knowing that this monthly review will occur works wonders. It almost always helps me stay within budget.

I like to spend money on books, for instance, so I have a monthly budget for such purchases. When I see a new book I want to purchase, and then see that it costs more than the month's remaining budget allows, I typically wait another month to purchase it. Of course, I sometimes forget I really wanted that book by the start of the next month! Or I end up borrowing it from a friend or from our local library. The key is that I have a budget and use it. And if I don't, I've given my wife permission to gently chide me for spending too much.

My wife doesn't like me to mention this next fact, but—based on my life expectancy—I know I have a good chance of dying before she does. I also know that one of my responsibilities as a husband is to make sure my wife is taken care of and has the necessary knowledge to make effective financial decisions after I depart this world.

In my case, my wife would rather go to the dentist than review our budget. Nevertheless, we put forth the effort and take the time to both understand where we are financially and decide together how to pay the bills we receive each month. Over time, we've set up most of our bills to be paid electronically, which saves us several dollars on postage each month.

I know that I need to make sure there is enough money in our checking account each month to cover these automatic payments. If my spouse does not know this, however, and something were to happen to me, she could quickly run into major problems. This sounds hypothetical, but it happens to new widows and widowers all the time.

> **PRACTICAL EXAMPLE**
>
> *One of my clients called to tell me that his wife had just died. Unfortunately, his spouse had never taken the time to train him in their finances. He had no idea what to do. While the husband often dies first, there is a chance it may the wife. Lesson learned: wives need to train their husbands!*

Key 4: Keep Track of All of Your Expenses

Many miss this important concept during the initial stages of the budgeting process. You need to make sure you have a budgeting system that allows you to record everything. And then you need to actually do it!

Often when I meet with individuals to go over their budget, they will assure me that they're listing all of their expenses. But when we study the numbers, they often have a large surplus of funds on paper at the end of each month. In reality, though, they are going further into debt each month. The problem usually is their "MISCellaneous" category, which is another name for "Money I Spent Carelessly." Please make sure there is no such category in your budget!

In order to ensure that you are accurately recording all of your financial transactions (not just the ones in your checkbook), you need to record every penny you spend for the next 30 days. To accurately record these transactions, be sure to use Worksheet 10 in the back of this book.

Recording all of your expenses for a month may sound a bit challenging, but it's the only way you'll know with certainty whether you are staying on track with your budget.

Key 5: Develop a Reasonable Lifestyle

Some people live according to the principle that life is meant to be enjoyed and will use whatever money is necessary to live life to the fullest. For others, on the opposite end of the spectrum, frugality is the rule, saving for the future is what is important, and any enjoyment of life that costs money is out of the question.

So, what is a reasonable lifestyle? To begin with, it's certainly one you can afford.

Although the components of a reasonable lifestyle may vary, we must develop a lifestyle in which we live within our means. It's unreasonable to attempt to enjoy a $120,000 per year lifestyle if you make only $35,000 a year. I often tell my clients, "It's time to act your wage."

In our status-conscious society, however, we often incorrectly believe that we are the only ones who don't have something. Easy credit and the ease of accumulating debt seem like bridges. Sure, they allow us to enjoy a more expensive lifestyle for a season or two. After a while we almost start believing "we can have it all now." But after it's too late, we discover that easy credit and debt are trap doors to financial disaster.

All of us should enjoy this life, but we must do so at a level commensurate with our current wages.

Two inescapable questions:

- Is your current lifestyle reasonable, based on your level of income?
- Are you maximizing your resources, or are you honoring yourself in a vain attempt to feel more successful?

> **PRACTICAL EXAMPLE**
>
> *George and Phyllis currently have $8,000 in credit card debt. If they make the minimum payments at 18 percent, it will take 25 years to pay it off, and they will end up paying $24,000.*

Key 6: Know When to Say Enough Is Enough

How often do we look in our closets and complain that we don't have a thing to wear, and in our cupboards or refrigerators and say we have nothing to eat . . . even though both are stuffed to capacity!? What we're really saying is that nothing jumps out at us, we're too lazy to look or cook, or nothing suits our fancy at the moment.

Contentment with what we currently have is a marvelous strength. By exercising this strength we avoid or rid ourselves of untold problems and develop an amazing sense of freedom, joy, and relief. If we learn to say that what we have today is enough, we'll be happier for years to come.

> **PRACTICAL EXAMPLE**
>
> *The size of the average American home has grown over the past quarter of a century from under 1,500 square feet to more than 2,000 square feet of living space. Much of this extra space comes from enlarged kitchens and multiple baths. Ironically, we still don't have enough space to hold all of our stuff.*

Key 7: Develop an 80/20 Mentality

Most people know and can apply the 80/20 principle. If you are a manager, you know that 80 percent of your problems are caused by 20 percent of your employees. If you are in business or in sales, you know that 80 percent of your revenue comes from 20 percent of your customers.

This 80/20 principle also applies to our finances. It means living on 80 percent of what we make so we can have a margin or cushion to cover the unexpected and make necessary investments for our future. I know a number of people who use the 20% to invest in savings and invest in themselves so they become more valuable in the future.

How much better to live by the 80/20 principle than to spend 100 percent or more of what we make every month, creating more burdens than we care to admit.

What budget cuts do you project you need to make in order to live by this rule?

Budgeting Systems

In the previous section we listed a number of keys to consider when we set up our budgeting system. Now we will look at a number of budgeting systems that will allow us to manage our finances effectively. Without these systems we will constantly wonder where our money went.

The basic systems described in the following pages work effectively for most people. We all have different needs and abilities, though, when it comes to managing our finances. If one of these systems works, great! If it doesn't, we need to remember one of the first keys: identify the parts that are not working for us and modify the system to address these issues. Developing a system that will meet our overall needs is very important, so we need to continue to make progress with the system we're using and not give up. When I first started preparing a budget for my own family, it quickly became clear that I needed to make some adjustments. Modify your budget system until it's truly yours.

Our household budgeting system continues to evolve as our lives change. You'll probably need to do the same with your system. In case you don't already have one, here is a brief explanation of the three most common budgeting systems.

Envelope Systems

To set up this type of system you simply take a stack of envelopes and label them with the names of all the categories you want to track.

When you get paid, you take predetermined amounts of cash and put them into the various envelopes. When you need to pay a bill, you simply go to the respective envelope and take out the money necessary to pay it. If you want to go out for pizza and a movie on Friday night, you simply check your entertainment envelope. If it has only a few dollars left, you make other plans.

Watch out for the temptation to rob your utilities envelope so you can enjoy a night out, thinking you'll be able to pay back the money later. That's often not the case, and you'll end up short when it comes time to pay your electric bill. What goes into a given envelope stays in that envelope until it's time to pay that particular bill.

If you decide to use this system, create envelopes only for the major budget categories. In the past I have worked with individuals using 50, 100, or even 150+ different envelopes. It's almost impossible to maintain such a system. Keep your envelope system as simple as possible.

The benefits of the envelope system include being simple and easy to use. It also provides you with a level of tangible control over your finances.

A common disadvantage of this system is the failure to create and fund envelopes for savings and longer-range variable expenses.

Modified Envelope Systems

With the modified envelope system, you deposit your paycheck into a checking account and then divide the amount of your check into both normal monthly and variable categories.

You can create additional worksheets to assist in further dividing these amounts into various subcategories based on the percentages you determined during the budget process. You then simply record the various monthly amounts on individual account pages and diligently keep track of what you spend. Think of each payment as a withdrawal from an individual account page. At the end of each month remove any remaining balances from your individual account pages and add them to the account savings page.

Let's suppose you were planning to go out on Friday. With the modified envelope system you would simply look at your account page to see what amount you have available within this category.

In addition, as you pay your variable expenses, you can if necessary move funds from your account savings pages to your individual account pages to pay your bills.

When you receive your monthly account statement from your bank, you can use the check account reconciliation worksheet to make sure the amounts you have in your system balance with the amounts recorded at the bank.

Although this modified envelope system may seem a bit complicated or labor intensive, it shouldn't take much time before you are recording transactions like a pro. Maintaining this system should not require more than an hour per week.

This system has a number of advantages, including being fairly simple to use and providing a high level of control (as you record all of your expenses and keep all of your balances readily at hand on individual account pages). For these reasons, it should meet the budgeting needs of most individuals and households today.

Using Technology (Software)

As you continue to develop your budget, you may want to use electronic tools or web-based systems to help you record your transactions faster and to provide real-time feedback about the balances in each of your accounts. These electronic tools help reduce errors and also can provide feedback concerning the performance of your investment accounts.

With these systems you can generate and print a variety of expense, savings, budget, and investment reports that will help ensure that your budget stays on track. In addition, these systems are especially helpful in identifying specific kinds of expenses during tax season.

Most people who opt to use electronic budgeting select Quicken or Mint, which are both produced from Intuit Inc. This program is updated annually and provides a number of electronic links to financial institutions, which can eliminate the need to manually record all of your transactions. There are a number of versions, from basic to advanced. Software programs have unique advantages and are excellent in providing you with the necessary tools to effectively manage your personal finances.

Other options include a new group of web-based financial programs. The advantages of an online system include being able to access your information anywhere, being able to link the software to financial institutions for real-time updates, and having all of your financial data backed up on a regular basis.

Still, there are some downsides. Having all of your financial data on a remote system doesn't help if you are in an area that doesn't have high-speed internet connectivity readily available. There is also the potential risk that the hosting company could "data mine" your financial information. So choose wisely.

If you're just getting started, it may be wise for you to start out with a manual system. Once you get your finances under control, you can decide whether to move to one of the electronic systems.

Defining Needs vs. Wants

As you continue to develop your budget, be sure you understand the difference between needs and wants. Some goals involve necessities for our survival; others are simply things we would like to have or do. Retirement or funding our children's education may seem like a need, but more likely it falls into the want category. We desire to fund our wants, but we need to ensure that we have the resources to fund our more important and needful goals before we use limited financial resources for non-necessities.

Knowing Your Financial Condition in Six Easy Steps

The six steps we will walk through today will expand on our work from the previous session and, although relatively simple to complete, will reveal quite a bit about your current financial condition. The six steps include identifying the variable expenses of your household, listing your total monthly income and expenses, verifying your monthly expenses, compiling a comprehensive list of all current debts, and preparing a set of personal financial statements.

These six steps may seem a bit overwhelming at first, and you may feel as though you don't have the necessary skills to complete the worksheets on your own. However, the only skills required involve basic addition and subtraction, along with a knowledge of how to fill in boxes on various forms. Be assured that you have all the skills required to complete these exercises. Taking them one step at a time will make their completion more manageable.

Let's start working through the tasks together.

Step One: Identification of Variable Income and Expenses

The first step, which we have already completed, was to identify your household's variable income and expenses. It is relatively easy to identify a household's recurring income and expenses. It is more difficult to identify income and expenses that occur only one or more times per year.

Examples of variable income payments include bonuses received at work and tax refunds. The average American receives an annual refund of approximately $2,700. Most individuals use these refunds to catch up on overdue bills, make additional payments toward debt reduction, or make one-time annual splurges on clothing or other larger purchases. The sad part is that while people receive these refunds after their annual tax returns are filed, they often pay extra to receive them in an expedited manner. These overpayments constitute interest-free loans to the government. Instead, make the necessary arrangements to receive more take-home pay each month, which will help you balance your monthly budget.

Examples of variable expenses include automobile insurance and Christmas presents. The average household spends $1,200 for Christmas presents each year. If you broke this down into a regular expense, you would need to budget $100 per month, more than most people can probably afford. So where are these funds coming from? In most cases they're coming from increasing debt, primarily through the use of credit cards.

> **TRANSFORMATIONAL TIP**
>
> *Many Americans purchase Christmas presents assuming they will have the money in January to pay these bills. However, when one looks at all of the other expenses during the holidays, this payback rarely occurs, and households begin the year already further behind financially. Instead, make plans to enjoy Christmas more while spending less.*

In the case of automobile insurance, one often pays these expenses in advance for the next six months. If one does not plan for these semi-annual expenses, it may be difficult to find the funds necessary to pay for these periodic bills.

It is important to take the time to complete this step fully before moving on, as the accuracy of your next step will be directly related to your accuracy with this one. If you are married, spend some time with your spouse to complete this exercise. If you are single, you may want to ask someone to help you during this process and to serve as an accountability partner.

As you list future variable expenses, you may not know exactly how much you are going to spend on this year's vacation or Christmas presents. If that's the case, you may want to look back at last year's expenses as guides for determining what you might spend this year.

In order to substantially reduce the stresses and financial pressures that plague your life, and to greatly increase your peace and contentment, stop reading and complete Step One before moving on. Believe me, you'll be glad you did! After all, you're beginning an exciting, transformative journey!

> ### PRACTICAL EXAMPLE
>
> *Bill and Mary spend on average $600 for Christmas presents in December, $200 for back-to-school items in August, $300 for dentists in November, $100 for birthday presents in March, and $1,200 for a family vacation in June. In addition, they pay $1,150 for property taxes in September and $50 more in February. The total of all these variable expenses is $3,600 per year. To cover all of these items, the couple will need to factor $300 into their monthly budgets.*

Step Two: Completion of a Projected Monthly Budget Statement

The second step is identifying your regular and recurring monthly income and expenses. This worksheet includes a number of income and expense categories and subcategories. It is important that you enter these amounts as accurately as possible. Again, asking a spouse or friend to work with you may be helpful.

As you complete Step Two, be sure to report your actual income and expenses. Don't report what you would like them to be, or what you hope they will be after making some adjustments, or what might be the case after you receive that new position at work.

To increase the accuracy of your figures, you may want to go back a few months in your financial records and compute monthly averages. Of course, a number of expenses will be easy to compute, including your mortgage or car payment. More variable expenses, such as food, entertainment, and recreation, will be accurate only if you average your actual expenses over the past few months. If you are still unsure what to report in a given category, use your best guess. Then again, for some categories you'll simply enter zero.

The goal of Step Two is to prepare a financial statement that shows your typical monthly cash inflow and outflow. This important step often results in one or more "Aha!" moments.

> ### PRACTICAL EXAMPLE
> *Mike and Sharron, along with their three children, live a relatively simple life. Mike and Sharron each makes $3,000 per month, and after taxes they take home a joint income of approximately $4,500. Their major expenses include $1,500 for their mortgage, $1,000 for two car lease payments and fuel, $200 for insurance, $500 for food, $150 for cable and cell phones, $200 for utilities, $200 for entertainment, and $750 per month in childcare for their three children. Based on these numbers, while their monthly income is $4,500 their expenses also total $4,500 per month, leaving them with no monthly surplus. Still, Mike would like to upgrade their cable service and take the family on a vacation next year. Sharron would like to start putting money away for retirement. Based on their current level of spending, however, the couple cannot do any additional spending without going into debt. In addition, they cannot build any savings to cover an unexpected expense, such as an appliance breaking down or their cars needing repairs. Even though they are able to pay their current bills, this couple needs to make some spending cuts in order to better position themselves for the future.*

If you live in a two-income household, it can be fascinating to identify the income generated by each spouse and then to record both the income and the work-related expenses of the lower-income spouse on a separate sheet.

Throughout the past 25 years I have talked with many two-income couples who claim that one of them would love to stay at home while the children are young but then insist that this would be impossible because of their financial needs. By removing all of the expenses for a two-income household, however—including having two cars, one's business wardrobe, daycare for the children, and prepared meals—the net income of a dual-income household usually is much less than they would have guessed.

When one computes the true net earnings for each spouse, the lower-income spouse often works for only a dollar or two an hour. As a result, making the change to a single-income family is usually not difficult.

Those who receive variable income, including commissioned salespersons, often find it difficult to determine their average monthly income. To begin, take your W-2 income for the past year and divide it by 12 to compute a monthly average.

Of course, this year's projected earnings, based upon last year's averages, will be only as accurate as this year's monthly incomes are similar to last year's. One must continually watch her earnings trends and make monthly or quarterly comparisons with past years. If your income so far this year is significantly lower than last year's, you need to make corresponding adjustments to this year's income statement and related expenses.

Whatever you do, be careful during good times. Absolutely refuse to adopt a "this will never change" attitude, and certainly don't allow your standard of living to exceed what your "normal" average earnings can support. Otherwise, the next economic downturn will trip you up and force you to significantly lower your standard of living.

> ### PRACTICAL EXAMPLE
>
> *Bob is a mortgage broker with ABC Mortgage and receives commissions based solely on his performance. Bob made $2,000 last month and $6,000 the month before that. During the first quarter of last year Bob's income topped $25,000, but his annual income came in close to $72,000. During the first quarter of this year his total income was $18,000, or a decrease of 28 percent from last year's. As a result, Bob should start budgeting at an income level that is 72 percent of what he made last year and reduce his expenses accordingly.*

After you have entered amounts into the various income and expense categories, add everything up. Then subtract your expenses from your income to arrive at an accurate picture of how you're doing.

If your worksheet says you have a monthly surplus, you may be quite proud of yourself. When working with individuals and couples in this situation, however, I often ask a basic question: "Are you telling me that at the end of each month you always have money that you don't know what to do with?"

The response I usually get is that they not only don't have any surplus funds at month's end but are consistently falling short.

If this is true of you, go back over the facts and figures you listed on Worksheet 2. What figures need to be double-checked? What facts did you forget to list? Among other things, how much "petty cash" do you carry in your wallet or purse each week? What unrecorded expenses are listed on your monthly credit card statements for the past three months? Even small things like your daily latte, mocha, or cappuccino can add $100 or more every month.

If you are in a deficit situation, don't forget that you are not alone. Most households overspend on a regular basis. If you could look closely at the financial records of individuals you believe are wealthy, you probably would discover that they are simply carrying higher amounts of debt than you are. The true millionaires are average people who enjoy a simple, but contented, lifestyle.

Again, it is important that you have a good handle on your monthly expenses before moving to Step Three. Reading about these concepts without filling out the worksheets will do nothing to change your financial future. Then again, you could start saving thousands of dollars between now and New Year's Day. Go for it!

Step Three: Verifying the Monthly Statement

The figures you listed on Worksheet 2 may not be entirely accurate. So, while you continue working through all of the steps in this book, begin keeping a record of all the expenses you have. After you finish this week, keep recording your expenses for another 24 days. This may sound like a lot of busywork, but you'll be so glad you didn't skip this step.

Within the next month you'll probably discover a few items you need to add or correct to make the budget worksheet more accurate. Along the way you also may discover a few spending habits you didn't realize you (and your spouse) have. Resist the temptation to assign blame. Instead, congratulate yourself for going the extra mile!

Later this week, and again next month, you can decide what spending habits you want to change. The more you learn during Step Three, the faster you'll be able to pursue peace of mind and greater financial freedom.

Unlike most steps, this one is ongoing. So take two minutes to record any receipts you've received today and promise yourself that you'll do the same tomorrow.

Then keep moving forward!

Step Four: Listing Your Assets

One of the tasks we completed in the last session was to identify and list your assets, debts, and resulting equity. An asset is anything you own. Assets include such tangible items as your house, your clothes, your jewelry, your cars, your exercise equipment, your music collection, and other possessions that have monetary value. Assets also include such intangible items as bank, savings, retirement, and investment accounts. The estimated value of some of your larger assets, including your house, may be fairly easy to determine. But many smaller dollar figures you list will need to be educated guesses. Don't think in terms of rock bottom garage sale prices for smaller items. Instead, determine what you probably could get for the item on eBay. In every case, list the current value, not what you paid for the item. Normally you would list the assets on this worksheet by their relative liquidity, including the most liquid of all assets, your personal checking and savings accounts. Items you would not include on this worksheet include leased vehicles and term life insurance policies, since neither is a form of ownership.

If you have a whole life or universal life insurance policy, you can include the cash value of the policy as an asset. If you aren't sure of the cash value, you may want to contact the life insurance agent who sold you the policy.

As you list your assets, remember that vehicles depreciate quickly, and in some cases you may owe more than the car is worth. The same may be true for your house. But don't factor in what you owe. Simply list the resale value in today's market.

When you have listed all of your assets, total them, smile, take a quick stretch break, and then proceed to the next step.

Step Five: Preparing a List of Current Debts

This step isn't quite as much fun, but it's definitely the easiest. Review Worksheet 1 you completed before and make sure to list all the individuals and companies to whom you owe money, including the actual amount owed and the interest rate being charged.

Examples include credit card debt, car loans, unpaid medical bills, student loans, property taxes, home loans, second mortgages, and home equity lines of credit. If you are unsure of the amount you owe, or the interest rate you're being charged, call the bank or company or look up your account online.

After you've finished compiling the facts and figures, you may want to rewrite the list on a new worksheet. This time, list all of your debts from the highest to the lowest interest rate. This prioritized list will be invaluable later on this week.

> ### PRACTICAL EXAMPLE
>
> *If you have three debts—a $70,000 mortgage at 7%, a $5,000 credit card debt at 23%, and a $2,000 department store debt at 15%—on the worksheet you would list the mortgage first, as it has the lowest interest rate, even though the department store has the lowest balance. However, when it comes time to pay them off, you would select the one with the lowest balance to pay off first.*

> **TRANSFORMATIONAL TIP**
>
> *If you have an overwhelming amount of debt, don't let false guilt, past hurt, or depression immobilize you. Recently I counseled a couple who listed debts to more than 150 different individuals, couples, and businesses. Almost 100 of the debts could have been satisfied with just $1,000. The couple had considered bankruptcy but, due to personal religious beliefs, could not bring themselves to file. Bear in mind that doing nothing doesn't work. You owe it to yourself to keep moving forward. Before this week is over you will have a realistic, clear-cut plan for reducing your debts, increasing your net worth, and enjoying life more.*

Step Six: Preparing a Personal Financial Statement

We're almost done! The next step is integrating some of the key numbers you've compiled for this session. Start by taking Worksheet 3, which lists your assets, and enter the total amount of debt listed there at the end of Worksheet 4. Now subtract that debt from your assets to arrive at your current net worth.

Don't be surprised if your current net worth is low or even negative. Thankfully, you've compiled other information you can use in coming days to substantially improve your net worth over time. Whatever you do, don't toss these worksheets. Instead, hang onto them as reminders of where you started on your journey to financial freedom.

Based on your work from the first session, and your commitment to keep reading, I'm confident that you're someone who desires to make positive and permanent financial changes.

If you agree, congratulations! You are well on your way toward financial freedom.

Balancing Your Budget and Creating a Margin for Goals

In this session we will also explore possible changes you can make to balance your budget and create financial margins that will enable you to save for the important life goals you identified in the previous session.

The sizes and types of financial changes you will need to make directly relate to your current financial status, which we determined together during the first session.

If your expenses are grossly out of balance with your income, you will need to make a number of significant changes to balance your accounts.

If you are slightly out of balance, the changes will be fewer and probably smaller. Still, you will need to make enough changes to enable you to build up your savings and fund some of your longer-range plans and goals.

The completion of this session's activities may require some creative thought, some compromises, and a possible lifestyle change or two. If you're married, do all you can to avoid disagreements with your spouse. Instead, keep an open mind as you consider possible options. You both need to put "everything on the table" and be able to talk openly as you brainstorm and weigh potential changes.

> ## PRACTICAL EXAMPLE
>
> *Bill and Susan have been married for about 15 years. Due to overspending by both individuals, they have built up $25,000 in credit card debt and are currently overspending in the amount of $500 per month. Bill is an avid fisherman and will not hear of getting rid of his fishing boat or any of the accessories he has accumulated over the years. Instead, he has directed Susan to stop spending so much for weekly groceries. He is requiring her to reduce grocery expenses by no less than 50 percent, because he is convinced this is where their true problem lies.*

The problems in this example are glaring, aren't they? Scenarios like this can cause serious disagreements, frustrations, and undue martial stress. Left unchecked, such financial stressors ultimately can lead to divorce. One recent study concluded that 90 percent of divorcing couples in the U.S. point to financial disagreements as one of the leading causes of their ruined marriage. Of course, divorce only compounds each person's financial woes. In reality, if a divorce occurs, the spending needed to support two households will almost double, adding to the financial stress, not taking it away. Individuals and couples in financial distress need to work together. Among other things, they need to explore whether other issues might be adding to their problems. If any session is going to cause disagreements, it will probably be this one. But it doesn't have to be that way.

If you are single, it may be wise for you to pair up with a good friend who can provide constructive criticism and independent advice as you review your spending patterns.

Carefully get ready for a life-changing session! Whatever you do, don't argue (even with yourself!), and don't stop reading.

Determining Necessary Changes

This part of the session is not just about cutting expenses but also about increasing our spending in other necessary areas, including giving, savings, and investments. The goal is not only to balance our budget but also to bring it in line with the plan we have created.

Determining which expenses to reduce or increase is a process that takes some time and careful reflection. It will also require us to identify which expenses are absolute necessities and which are nice but unnecessary for our survival. The absolutes need to be funded before niceties, preferences, and other discretionary items are even discussed.

In the next section we will begin to identify absolute necessities. Of course, many items that didn't even exist 5 or 10 years ago are often seen as today's "absolutes." In reality, if we did not have access to them for a while we might miss them, but we certainly could survive without them!

This past year my cell phone broke. I was told it would be cost-prohibitive to get it repaired since I was due to receive another free phone in two months. So I went without a cell phone temporarily. Normally I am a heavy cell phone user, and for the first few weeks I almost went through a form of withdrawal. After this initial shock wore off, however, I almost appreciated the silence and freedom of being "unavailable" at times. While I did get my brand-new cell phone at the end of two months, I knew it was no longer an absolute. If I wanted to, or if our budget was tight, I could get along just fine without one.

Breaking Down Absolute vs. Non-Absolute Expenses

Worksheet 11 in the back of this book will help you identify the financial absolutes and non-absolutes in your life.

Before going through this worksheet with your spouse or friend, take the time to fill it out on your own. This extra step may prevent a painful argument a few minutes from now.

> **REMEMBER**
>
> *An absolute expense is one we must incur each month for our survival. Examples include food, basic transportation, and rent or mortgage payments.*

A non-absolute expense is one that funds something we like to have but is not critical to our survival. This list includes a number of items we could give up if need be. Examples include cable television, cell phones, hobbies, and activities.

Take the time now to review your current monthly expenditures to determine whether each is an absolute or a non-absolute expense. In some cases you'll quickly identify items you can eliminate. Then review the other non-absolutes and ask yourself *Can I live without this, too?*

Resist the temptation, however, to rush out and cancel certain monthly expenses. Instead, simply identify possible cuts. Have some fun . . . but don't get ahead of yourself!

> ## PRACTICAL EXAMPLE
>
> *One of the fast-growing businesses in recent years has been that of self-storage warehouses. It never ceases to amaze me that people pay more than $75 per month to store $37.50 worth of stuff. While these goods may have been "necessities" at one point, today they are anything but. Getting rid of this clutter and junk may prove to be a very freeing experience. If anything, you can donate the useable stuff to the Salvation Army or Goodwill . . . and start saving a big chunk of money!*

Ideas for Balancing Your Budget

Now that you've finished the budget worksheet, it's time to consider all of the possible options to reduce your monthly expenses. Some non-absolutes can be eliminated with a simple phone call or letter. But be sure to look at additional ways to reduce your expenditures.

Some of the ideas listed below may work for you, while others may not. You certainly don't need to implement all of them, but you do need to identify several ways to increase your savings and give yourself the margin you need to fund your longer-term goals.

Telephone, Internet, Television: Find Ways to Trim Costs

Once amounting to a relatively small expense, telephone (including cell phones), internet access, and cable television costs have increased exponentially in the past few years. Although most of these expenses were once perceived as discretionary, most people now consider them necessities. Thankfully, there are a number of ways to reduce or eliminate these costs.

If everyone in the family has a cell phone, is there a real need for a home phone, too?

Does everyone in your household (including teenage children) really need to have a cell phone? Or can a limited number of phones be shared among your children?

Also, if you have multiple phones, are you on a family shared plan? Or have you shopped around to make sure you are getting the best rate based on the usage patterns within your family? Of course, watch out for low introductory rates that suddenly jump up in price and leave you locked in for two or more years.

You may want to give your kids prepaid cell phones with a fixed number of minutes.

Many children tend to spend endless hours with calls to friends and hundreds (or even thousands) of text messages. Having phones with limited minutes will cause your children to learn to live within a budget, while still giving you the peace of mind that they'll always have a phone handy in case of emergency.

> ### PRACTICAL EXAMPLE
>
> *As our children get older, all of them think they need a cell phone. After all, most high school students have one, and when my daughter was still 12, so did a number of her friends. Although as parents we want to be able to contact our children (and vice versa), the cost of each child having a cell phone is significant. One solution we use is a pay-as-you-go plan. The cost for cell phone service for my high school son, now that he pays it himself, has dropped from about $25 per month as an add-on to our family plan to only $80 per year as long as he stays within his allotted minutes. We love it because (a) he has a phone and (b) he is learning to wisely budget both his time and his money.*

Carefully budgeting telephone expenses isn't the only way to save money. If we need cable television, do we really need all of the premium channels? In our household we made the decision not to subscribe to cable television. Instead, we use an indoor television antenna. With it and the new digital system we can watch 15 channels at no cost. As an added bonus, we watch fewer hours of television and have found a number of other, more productive activities to pursue in our free time.

Those who find it difficult to give up their favorite television shows can do their homework and shop for competitive options and select the one with the lowest overall cost. Typically, cable services are highly competitive, offer many incentives, and allow you to negotiate cost reductions.

When it comes to internet service, most individuals, couples, and families can save a lot of money. We certainly don't need the fastest internet speed available for e-mail. In our family's case, the cost of switching to a lower speed was a painless cut that has saved us hundreds of dollars over the course of a year.

With the convergence of technologies, you may be able to combine (bundle) products and services to receive discounts from a single provider. If you have home phone service, check about getting cable service from the same provider. If you have cable, check about getting your internet service from the same company.

Before you finish this section, look at how much you're spending and ask yourself *Is this the best way to utilize our money? What is truly a need?* Although it may be difficult to give up some entertainment and communication options, it may just allow you more time with those you love.

> **PRACTICAL EXAMPLE**
>
> *While the costs of a new cell phone may seem quite attractive, by the time you add up all the provider charges, monthly service fees, and taxes the real cost can grow quickly. Also, before you enter into a long-term contract it is important to discuss all of the benefits and disadvantages and make sure you will have the money to pay for the service throughout the length of the contract.*

Groceries: Find Ways to Buy on Sale

Groceries are a necessary expenditure. Although food can be a relatively large monthly expense, there are plenty of ways to save money.

First, you can change where you shop. Where we shop can have a significant effect on our expenses. Low-cost food stores such as Aldi offer most food staples at a lower cost than fancier grocery store chains.

Second, you can purchase fewer premade dinners and make the same meals yourself. In two-income families, where time is often at a premium, purchasing meals at the grocery store's deli may save some time, but the meals cost a lot more.

A fun activity for your family may be to have a "Dinner Making Night." You can all take part making multiple supper entrees that can be frozen and then later popped into the oven or microwave. A benefit for Mom: your kids will be much more willing to eat what's for dinner!

Third, you can purchase rice and noodles and other basic food staples in bulk.

> **PRACTICAL EXAMPLE**
>
> *In a regular grocery store a bag of unpopped popcorn costs about $1 per pound. At a warehouse store, however, I can purchase 50 pounds of popcorn for $16. While I need to find appropriate storage for this and other bulk items, it does not take long for our family to start saving money.*

Fourth, you can use a grocery list when you shop. Grocers are particularly good marketers and will often offer a plethora of products they know you will want. Sure enough, you will buy them if you don't stick to your grocery list. By sticking to your list you will have a much greater chance of saving money week after week.

Fifth, when you build up a surplus in your grocery budget, use that surplus to purchase staple foods when they go on sale. Our family has built up quite a surplus in our food budget and can often take significant advantage of sales to purchase the items we use most.

Our family happens to eat an average of one can of corn weekly. So when the price of corn is marked down to $.40 cents per can from its usual $.75 per can, I purchase 52 cans of corn (thereby cutting our annual cost for this item by almost half).

> **PRACTICAL EXAMPLE**
>
> *Purchasing items on sale is not the only way to save on grocery bills. We often purchase our groceries in bulk (often from warehouse clubs) and split up the quantity among family and friends. By purchasing this way, we can purchase the items more often and all of us can realize the savings.*

Our family also frequently purchases large quantities of chicken and hamburger when they are on sale. Granted, stores often put limits on the number of items someone can purchase on sale, and they do this because of people like me!

When items go on sale, however, don't go overboard. You will achieve savings only if there is no risk of their spoiling before you use them.

> ### PRACTICAL EXAMPLE
>
> *For me, grocery shopping has become a game. Many grocery stores now list your purchase savings on each receipt. I don't feel as though I have had a successful grocery shopping experience unless the amount I have saved is more than the amount I have spent. I don't achieve this every time, of course, but I have done it often. You can, too.*

Christmas: Creative Gifts and Giving

The one time of year when most people overspend is Christmas. Although we all want to give gifts at Christmas, our tendency year after year is to spend too much. Knowing this, our family has one of two choices at Christmas.

First, we can stay within budget month after month and save the necessary money to purchase the items we want to give.

Second, if we didn't save enough money for lots of Christmas shopping, we either give fewer presents or make our own gifts.

As I look at all the Christmas presents I've given my children over the years, I realize that they've often been played with for only a few days and quickly forgotten.

A number of years ago, when my son was much younger, he often had more fun with the cardboard boxes the presents came in than with the presents themselves. Other parents have told me the same thing.

Furthermore, personal gifts created by us for our children may have more lasting value. I know many families who make this kind of giving a practice every year, and I applaud them for doing so. Often this is done out of necessity, but they're blessing their children by their creativity and careful stewardship of the money they have received. These ideas will hopefully provide a good example they can use for the rest of their lives.

True, many of us want to give exceptional presents to our children, especially when they are young. But taking on debt to do so can negatively affect our children for years to come.

Some critics go so far as to say that not spending excessively for Christmas presents is un-American, since many retailers depend on Christmas spending to carry them through the rest of the year. Still, you must consistently look at what is best for *your family* long term and not worry about how your small family's spending affects the overall economy.

> ### PRACTICAL EXAMPLE
>
> *Last year my younger daughter wanted a bed set for her American Girl doll that cost over $100 from the American Girl store. As I looked at the set in the catalog, it looked like just a few pieces of plastic put together with some fabric for the bedspread and canopy. My wife, who is rather creative, stated that she could easily make one of these. At Christmas my daughter received a bed set my wife had made that almost matched the one in the American Girl catalog. In fact, our daughter didn't even realize it wasn't the actual set until my wife told her that she had made it. Now my daughter treasures the bed set even more because it's the handiwork of her mom. Total cost for all of the materials to make the bed: $15. Savings: $85.*

Dining Out on a Budget

Can a family eat out periodically and still rein in their budget? I believe they can if they do the right things.

As everyone knows, the cost of eating out has risen significantly over the years. This is especially true now that my kids are too old to order from the children's menu. Still, I love to eat out and often look forward to trying new restaurants.

Here are a few ways we've found to save money:

First, my kids love to go to fast food hamburger restaurants, and most of them have a special or dollar menu. I love to watch the face of the clerk when we order 10 double cheeseburgers and 5 chicken sandwiches without fries or drinks. My son, who has a healthy appetite, gets plenty to eat without breaking the bank.

> **PRACTICAL EXAMPLE**
>
> *At some McDonald's restaurants the cost of a single cheeseburger is $.99, while the double is $1.00. I've also seen cases where a single hamburger costs more than the double cheeseburger, or 4 chicken nuggets cost $1.00 and six cost $2.79. These area no-brainers: order two 4-piece chicken nuggets, throw away the extra two nuggets, and still save $.79.*

Purchasing items on the low-cost menu can save you money as long as you don't fill up on all of the higher priced items. I remember on one visit to McDonald's when my kids were teenagers seeing the look of the clerk's face when I ordered 15 McChicken sandwiches.

Second, when our family goes out to eat we limit ourselves to certain items. Typically we do not purchase appetizers or desserts, either of which can cost almost as much as the meals. Instead of spending $20 for desserts, we go somewhere else and order sundaes from a dollar menu.

Nor do we order drinks in a restaurant. I am not referring to just alcoholic drinks, but also to soda. Purchasing a few glasses of soda can add $10 or $12 to our dining bill. At most restaurants we drink water, which is healthier than soda. We wait until we are home to enjoy two liters of ice-cold soda that cost us $.84 (purchased on sale).

Another strategy we use is couponing and taking advantage of other discount programs. We like to purchase an entertainment book for our area. Similar books are available in major cities across the United States, and part of the proceeds usually benefits a local organization. These entertainment books allow us to try a variety of restaurants at half their normal cost. When we select the restaurant for a particular evening, it is not unusual for us to take out our coupon book and page through it. Other services I have used include Restaurant.com, Entertainment books, or Groupon. This kind of service allows us to purchase gift certificates or half price or discounted meals. The cost is usually $10 for a $25 restaurant gift certificate. That certificate usually mandates that you purchase $35 of food in order to use it. When you open an account at Restaurant.com (which is free), you will often receive an e-mail that gives you a code telling you where you can purchase the gift certificates for 50 percent to 80 percent off. A $25 gift certificate can cost only $2 to $5, and a $35 restaurant bill will cost you only $13 to $15 total. Talk about a great deal!

By using these discount programs, I find that we eat out more often, we usually eat at a higher-class restaurant, and we can go out for less than the overall cost of many fast food options.

Clothing

Clothing costs have become a significant expense for many Americans. Our children are often accepted or shunned based on the clothing or labels they are wearing. Although it is important for our children to be accepted, it is also important that we be reasonable in this regard. There are a number of strategies that may help reduce our expenses in this area.

First, shop when things are on sale. Many stores have back-to-school specials, but the better time to purchase such items may be during an after-season closeout. This may be easier for some of us who have older children than for families with growing younger children.

Second, shop the garage sales of upper scale subdivisions. Many of these families purchased the name brand products you and your kids want and are selling them for a small fraction of what they paid for them. This way you or your kids can have the name brands and you can stay within your budget.

Third, you can shop at consignment or Goodwill stores. I have talked with a number of people who reported that the best clothing selection of the year takes place the week between Christmas and New Year's, during which good clothing can be picked up for a small fraction of its original value. It is during this time that older, but still good, clothing is thrown out to make room for the new clothing received as Christmas presents.

Finally, let's all start a trend toward generic. There is usually no difference in quality between a $15 shirt and a $55 logoed shirt, other than the status it potentially conveys. To stay within our budgets, we need to realize that a shirt is a shirt. We should not give in to a felt need to prove a status in life!

Making the Necessary Changes

We are now at the point where changes in your spending habits must be made. Although you may feel a little apprehensive about making some of these changes, this is the only way you can change your financial situation and move toward financial freedom.

In this section you looked at a number of possible ways you could change your budget, not only to balance it but also to develop surplus funds that can be allocated toward the longer-term goals you will be developing later this week.

Worksheet 6 in the back of this book will guide you in deciding which changes to make. This worksheet can be used as a guide to list possible budget reductions and the dollars you would save as a result. This process—though sometimes difficult—is necessary, significant, and worthwhile for you in the longer term. In many cases, though, you'll find this exercise exciting, and even exhilarating. Why? Because you'll enjoy the immediate satisfaction of making good, healthy financial choices that will pay substantive long-term dividends.

Remember that you need to eliminate overspending each month and then cut your expenses even further in order to build in a margin for unexpected expenses and accelerate the payoff of your debts.

As you go through this process, don't forget the adage "You can pay me now or later." If you want everything now (which has been America's motto for a generation), you will have to make substantive sacrifices later on—and possibly not have enough funds to support yourself in your later years. By making budget reductions now, you will experience increased contentment in the coming months and enjoy many more options later in life as well.

This is not an easy overall process, but it is my hope that it will give you a sense of peace in your life.

Creating a Balanced Budget

Now that you have identified all of the necessary budget changes, the time has come to put your new budget into action.

Although this may sound easy, the reality is that following through with these changes, and not reverting back to old ways, may be a difficult process for you. It may require significant dedication, some personal sacrifices, and compromises between spouses (if you're married). Worksheet 7 at the back of this book is a record of your previous levels of spending, the projected effects of the changes you have agreed to make, and your newly determined spending levels.

I want to reiterate that the goal is not just to achieve a balance between monthly income and expenses. You also want to create a surplus that can offset your debt and increase your savings.

You may want to save the completed Worksheet 7 for years to come so you can document the dramatic positive effects of the changes you're making today. Believe me, it will be fun for you to go back and see the progress you have made. And if you become discouraged anywhere along the way, you can always go back to this worksheet for encouragement.

Again, be sure to take the action steps necessary to make today's changes a permanent reality. Once your monthly income adequately exceeds your expenses, you can go on to the next section of this session's work.

The Problems with Debt

Debt seems to be a "normal" part of life today. Everywhere we look we see mountains of debt. The U.S. government borrows immense amounts of money every day. Corporations use debt to leverage their assets in order to create new competitive advantages. Millions of Americans use debt to finance everything from homes to cars and from vacations to electronics. Every day we acquire more stuff with money we don't even have.

The use of debt and credit cards to purchase things is a relatively new concept. The older generation used cash to purchase almost everything when they were younger. If they needed a washer or dryer, they saved up to pay for it. If they didn't have the money in savings, they went without until they did. Many cringe at the way most of us use debt today. Yet a majority of Americans believe that debt is helpful, and even good. Is this true?

I believe that the availability of debt has caused the prices of goods and services in many parts of this country to rise. Think what a home would cost today if you were able to secure only a five-year loan. The average price of homes would have to be a lot lower. Conversely, the availability of loans and other forms of credit has indirectly caused prices to inflate significantly over the past few decades.

Another problem with debt is the limit it can place on your future. This can happen in two ways: first, by spending today, you will not have the funds to spend on important and necessary items in the future. Second, by incurring debt and its related finance charges, the items you purchase will cost more over time than if you had paid cash.

I think we can all agree that using credit makes it much easier for us to purchase (1) things we do not need and (2) things we would not purchase if we had to use cash.

Even if we believe we can handle the debt load we currently have, we are still slaves to the lenders. If you don't believe this, try missing one or two car or house payments. If you do, you'll be at risk of losing your car or house, no matter how much you've already paid for them.

Shop Until We Drop?

For many people the experience of going to the mall to shop is just as much a sport as is hunting or fishing for others. For many, the experience of shopping is just that—an experience. They can spend the entire day looking at clothes without making many purchases. Others don't understand this, and within families and marriages this can cause a lot of frustration and outright conflict.

I like to joke that some men shop the same way they hunt. They go into one store, find their size quickly, purchase the item, and are out of the store within minutes. I can walk throughout an entire mall, return to the same store where I left my wife, and often find her just a few feet from where she had been standing before. How does she do that? It's beyond me.

Honestly, most of us already have too much stuff. We rent outside storage units at a considerable expense, only to store items of little economic value. Why do so many people feel the need to rent outside storage in the first place? Often it is because they have purchased so much new "stuff" that they can't fit it all into their already oversized, overstuffed homes. Why don't we just spend less, consume less, and be more content with what we have already?

If you're married, you and your spouse need to discuss who typically spends more. In the average family, the husband typically spends more than the wife. Women tend to shop more often but spend smaller amounts. Men usually shop less frequently but purchase much more expensive items, such as electronics, campers, boats, and sporting equipment. Then again, it can be the woman who has difficulty controlling her spending.

Regardless, one of you probably has a problem with spending. Don't be judgmental, as opposites frequently balance each other out in marriage. Once you identify the spender, you can review his or her spending patterns to determine the extent of the problem and how it usually occurs. For example, if the person typically overspends in particular stores, a simple answer may be to stay away from those stores.

PRACTICAL EXAMPLE

I often spend money on books. I know that if I go into a bookstore I will likely come out with a new book I probably will not have time to read. If I stay out of bookstores, I probably won't purchase any new books. Similarly, there is a certain clothing store that causes problems for my wife. Choosing where we do—and don't—shop helps both of us stay within budget.

Much of our economy is built on continued consumer consumption and ever-increasing levels of spending. However, if we continue to do what we have done in the past, we are going to continue to get the results we got in the past. Unless we choose to make changes, we are only going to get ourselves deeper and deeper into debt.

If you want to change your financial future, you must begin to eradicate some of your past behaviors. Thankfully, when you begin to do things differently, you begin to experience significant benefits. One benefit is the satisfaction of knowing *I'm making the right choice again*. It feels good! Be sure to follow through on the positive financial choices you're making this week.

Credit Cards

People who use credit cards regularly spend 30 percent more using those cards than they would if they paid with cash. Retailers know this, which is why so many of them not only allow but encourage you to use credit cards. Besides, it seems easier and more convenient to pull out your plastic and use it.

So, are credit cards all bad? No.

One of the ways credit cards can be used effectively is to use them for budgeted expenses only. That way it's always a planned purchase you already know is in the budget.

Another way is to take out your checkbook each time you use your credit card and subtract the amount of the transaction from your checking account. Then when you receive the credit card bill you'll already have the money needed to pay it all off. Of course, this will work only if you make sure you write down every credit card transaction in your checkbook.

A simpler approach is to use a debit card instead of a credit card, which will remove the money from your checking account when each transaction happens.

There are times when credit cards speed up the process or provide other benefits. Just try renting a car without a credit card or making a hotel reservation in a distant city. In addition, if you travel overseas, you'll find that using a credit card for purchases or cash advances from foreign ATM machines often provides some of the best exchange rates.

In today's increasingly complex financial environment, banks are finding it easier to add additional fees and charges, including late fees and over-the-limit fees, and even resorting to changing the date or time a payment is due to cause it to be late. I find it amusing that banks typically call a responsible spender who pays off her card balances each month a "deadbeat"!

In one case a card company issued multiple low-credit-limit cards to individuals and then began charging them multiple times for late fees and over-limit fees on top of exorbitantly high interest rates. The individual taken advantage of in this way had to pay more than $400 in over-limit fees alone.

Credit cards often seem to offer access to easy money. They appear to provide funds to do things or purchase items you can't yet afford. But of course, that's an illusion. Promise yourself that you'll never spend money you don't have.

PRACTICAL EXAMPLE

Wally and Sarah have decided to take their children on a family vacation. They use their credit cards throughout the vacation—and when they return discover they've spent $2,400.00. They have allotted $50 per month in their budget for vacations and travel. They had hoped to take another vacation in two years, but if they pay the $50 a month at 18 percent interest, it will take them almost seven years to pay off this first trip.

> **PRACTICAL EXAMPLE**
>
> *Sam and Mary needed a new roof for their home. They knew that the home would eventually need a new roof, but they did not save over time for this cost. The cost of the roof was $4,500, "paid for" with credit cards. At $70 per month, it will take the couple 16 years to pay off that necessary but costly expenditure. By the time they finally pay it off, it may be time for Sam and Mary to hire someone to replace their roof again. Paying $70 per month for 16 years would actually amount to a total expense of $13,440 for a $4,500 roof.*

Again, using credit cards wisely can offer a number of benefits. You can earn miles or points that can be used for airline travel, hotel stays, and merchandise. These are true benefits, though, only if you use the cards for budgeted items, you pay off the entire balance each month, and the card doesn't charge interest if you don't carry any balance into a second month.

If you ever maintain a credit card balance, or fail to pay your bill on time, the interest and fees you'll end up paying will far outweigh the benefits of any mileage points you might receive.

For many years now leading financial authors have been writing about the evils of credit cards. Though using credit cards involves many dangers, credit cards themselves are not the problem. The real problem is always the unwise user.

I am often asked whether it is wise to take advantage of the many credit cards that offer cheap interest rates, or to use cards that use substantive interest rate reductions as introductory offers. Yes, I believe these offers can be used to reduce our interest and allow us to pay off our credit debt at a faster rate. One needs to be careful, however, of the interest rate charged after the introductory period. Never fall into the trap of continuing to use the card at the higher rate.

Although it may look good for you to be able to pay off your MasterCard with your Visa, in the long run you need to pay off all credit card debt. You'll be so glad you did.

Buying Too Much House

The problem for many is not purchasing a house that has too much square footage but buying one that is too expensive in relation to their income. A generation ago many families lived in a home with one bathroom for five kids and a one-stall garage for the family car. Today, a bathroom for every person is often considered a "must," and a three-stall garage seems to be a necessity.

Home ownership with its associated taxes and maintenance costs is expensive. Sadly, many families do not consider the total cost of home ownership before making this lifestyle decision. In addition, problems arise when we want to purchase a home in a desirable neighborhood and this stretches a family's budget to the point that both husband and wife need to work. But the facts on the ground remain the same.

Time is one of the most precious commodities we have, and our kids grow up so quickly. Wouldn't it be better to live in a smaller house so we can have a bigger allotment of time together as a family?

Of course, family time isn't the only thing that can be lost in this situation. John and Rebekah don't have any children yet, but their situation, below, is more common than you might imagine.

> **PRACTICAL EXAMPLE**
>
> *John purchased a home in a rather prestigious subdivision. Unfortunately, making the monthly payments was difficult for him, and he could not afford to furnish much of the home. Both John and his wife, Rebekah, were working two jobs so they could keep the home of their dreams. They noticed that many couples in their subdivision were divorcing and that some of the homes were going into foreclosure. Those couples were obviously facing similar financial struggles.*

The Refinancing Trap

Decreases in interest rates often fuel significant increases in the number of home refinances. The lowering of interest rates is a significant benefit to the budgets of many, as it allows them to reduce their monthly home payments. That's great. What's not great is how many people add to the amount of their loan so they can purchase more "stuff" with the additional funds.

When I refinanced my home recently, I was given the opportunity to borrow an additional $10,000, which I declined to do. However, when I received the loan check it included this additional $10,000. I believe that most people would have simply taken this money and purchased a new fishing boat or taken a "needed" vacation. The more prudent thing to do, however, would be to take this amount and pay it right back on the principle of the loan.

When interest rates are lower, we can normally purchase a larger home at a smaller monthly payment than when interest rates are higher. Over the past few years many households have refinanced their home a number of times to take advantage of these lower interest rates.

Some individuals are locked into a 30-year fixed rate, but many others have opted for adjustable rate mortgages (ARM), which offer a lower interest rate and lower monthly payments—at least initially. Sadly, most are caught off guard when interest rates rise—and their monthly payments rise significantly, too. Such drastic cost increases have resulted in millions of loan defaults, especially in sub-prime markets.

It's absolutely critical that we make wise choices when it comes to purchasing a home. Each choice could end up wasting or saving literally tens of thousands of dollars.

PRACTICAL EXAMPLE

Simon and Sharon purchased their $175,000 home 10 years ago on a 30-year mortgage at a fixed interest rate of 10 percent. At this rate their monthly payment was $1,523.06, and the final cost of their home after 30 years would be $548,301 ($1,523.06 times 12 payments per year times 30 years). After 10 years of payments they determined they still owed $127,792.54. Due to the changing economic environment, they had the opportunity to refinance and set up a new 30-year loan at 6 percent. This would reduce their monthly payments to $762.37 per month, which would be a savings of $760.69 per month. Although they could use this savings to increase spending in other areas, if they continued to make the larger monthly payments already factored into their budget they could completely pay off their house in 9 years and save more than $191,000 in interest costs.

Buying Instead of Renting

It's the American dream to purchase a home, and many individuals want to build equity instead of pouring rental payments "down the drain." Even though current interest rates are relatively low, one must carefully consider whether it is wise to purchase a home in this economic environment.

Before you move from renting to purchasing a home, or before you purchase a larger or second home, you need to consider a number of factors. These include your current age and life stage, your current financial position, and the location of the home.

If you are younger, it may be wise to rent until you know exactly where you will be settling down. Many who have taken advantage of low interest rates to purchase a newer or larger home have found it difficult to sell their old house. Also, various parts of the country continue to experience economic difficulties, and selling homes in these areas has become a difficult and costly experience.

PRACTICAL EXAMPLE

Jamie, age 21, is a recent college graduate paying $650 per month for an apartment. Based on current interest rate levels, she thinks she could afford a home for the same monthly payment and is strongly considering a purchase. She currently has a few job prospects and a boyfriend in another city. Wisdom says that Jamie would be better off renting for at least two or three more years until she is sure of where she will end up in terms of a job and where she plans to settle down.

Is It Location, Location, Location?

One of the major factors in home selection is location. Location is important for a number of reasons, including the quality of education available for your children, the convenience in getting to places such as school and church, and (most importantly) your ability to sell the home in the future at a profit.

To sell your home at a profit, you need to look at what will constitute a good location in the future. Although some communities have an excellent future because of current global trends, others are near economically challenged areas, which could hamper your ability to sell your house, let alone for a profit.

Among other things, you need to study population movement and growth trends. As the Baby Boomer population ages, more people are moving toward southern and coastal regions. Currently, two-thirds of the United States population lives within 100 miles of the Atlantic Ocean, the Pacific Ocean, or the southern border of the United States.

Over the next few years it may be much wiser to purchase a home in a population growth zone rather than in a region within the "Rust Belt" that already has suffered significant economic damage and decline.

Autos

The love of the automobile has long been associated with the American dream. The automobile, once a means of getting from one place to another, has become a symbol of status or affluence. Of course, as autos become pricier the monthly payments on them also have increased significantly.

In addition, we live in an environment in which many families cannot operate with only one car. Most people live in areas with, at best, only minimally adequate public transportation systems.

Beyond that, most family members who are able to drive now "require" a car for their sense of independence.

This section will expand on the various components of this budget buster and give you some concrete suggestions on how to move from financial bondage to contentment and success.

Choosing the Auto That Best Meets Your Needs

When you select a car that best suits your needs, remember that today's cars last longer than in the past. So be sure to keep your future needs in mind. Also, be sure to review the total costs of ownership. Your goal should be to lease or purchase the car that provides the largest return per thousand dollars. Make sure you fully factor in the costs of maintenance and insurance.

As you look at all the great automobiles available today, keep in mind that the basic purpose of an auto is to get you from point A to point B. We come equipped with two feet to do precisely the same thing, and any alternative mode of ambulation beyond our feet is simply a matter of speed and convenience. However, most Americans focus more on form and function, style and status than on the basic principle that cars transport us from A to B.

Recently someone told me about a friend who drives a jet-black BMW 750i with the vanity license plate "WAS HIS." The woman received it as part of their divorce settlement. Considering the cost of this vehicle, I think a more apt license plate would read "THE BNKS."

Honestly ask yourself three questions:

- "Am I using cars to make myself feel more important or to make others feel jealous?"
- "Do I believe that the more expensive the car I drive the more successful I must be?"
- "Is this the best use of my limited financial resources?"

Performing Appropriate Maintenance

The cars and trucks produced today are built better than ever, which means that they can last many years longer than previous models—if you take the time to maintain them properly. If you follow your car's recommended maintenance schedule you will usually avoid costly problems later on. One of the simplest and least expensive requirements is regular oil changes. But make sure you know what else your car needs—and when.

Should You Purchase New or Used?

I have often heard people say that when you purchase a used car you're purchasing someone else's problems. Years ago I would have agreed with this, but not anymore. As previously noted, cars generally last much longer than they did in the past. Also, large numbers of cars are leased on three-year contracts, which creates many excellent opportunities for individuals to purchase used cars with relatively low mileage.

In addition, so much of the depreciation of the vehicle's value occurs within the first few months. Several thousand dollars of resale value can be lost by simply driving a new car off the lot. For some, the experience of being able to drive a new vehicle, with all of the associated "new car smells," is something they value and can afford. Still, aren't there better ways to invest your money?

Because most auto depreciation occurs within the first 30 months, it is often best to purchase a vehicle that's between two-and-a-half and four years old. Purchasing a vehicle at the lowest cost versus benefit ratio is a wise choice every time.

Another benefit of purchasing a used vehicle is that it allows you to own a car that might ordinarily have been out of your price range. It's the best of both worlds. You have the opportunity to drive the make and model you want at a price you can afford.

For example, if you want to drive a Lexus or a BMW, purchasing one that is a few years old can shave off half of the cost or more, which could put the car into a price range you can afford.

The Leasing Trap

Leasing has become a more popular option in recent years. However, there are a number of pros and cons to consider before entering into a lease agreement.

In general, leasing has allowed the American consumer to drive a more expensive car than he or she could have afforded if it had been purchased with cash or with a loan.

Leasing has also allowed auto manufacturers to increase their profits by adding many expensive options, which considerably increase the overall price of the car. These price increases are not generally noticed by the average consumer, as she is usually concerned only about the monthly cost.

Many people argue that they will have to make car payments whether they purchase the car or lease it—so what's the problem with leasing? But is a monthly car payment always necessary? This mindset has contributed greatly to the financially stressed situation many are experiencing today. Having a never-ending monthly auto payment is not a recommended way of using our financial resources.

A few years ago I took the plunge and leased a very nice new car. I leased this vehicle because the company at which I was employed gave me a monthly car allowance. It was expected that, in my position, this car would be traded in every three years.

When I leased this car I looked at two vehicles. The calculated residual value of one of the cars was higher than that of the other. Even though the purchase price was higher, the monthly lease payment for this car was lower.

Due to the high mileage I was putting on each year, I purchased a lease with a much higher amount of allowable mileage. This higher mileage almost doubled my monthly payments but saved me a considerable amount at the end of the lease. I was allowed 60,000 miles during the three-year lease period. When I turned in the vehicle it had 60,043 miles on it, so I ended up paying only $4.30 in additional fees. Often these additional mileage fees are not anticipated and can cause hundreds or thousands of dollars of extra expenses at the end of the lease.

When I turned in my leased vehicle, I wondered whether I should purchase the vehicle for the residual value of the lease. The dealer mentioned, however, that there were other, comparable cars on the lot selling for three thousand less than my residual value. In effect, my leasing this vehicle saved me three thousand dollars.

Based on my own experience, I have identified three important factors to consider before entering into a lease agreement. First, find a vehicle with the best lease cost, not the lowest purchase price. Second, purchase a plan with a high enough allowable mileage to meet your driving needs. Third, select a vehicle that will have a higher residual value than a comparable model at the expiration date of the lease.

Looked at this way, is leasing all that bad? It depends on the goals of the purchaser. If your employer requires you to change vehicles frequently, leasing may be an excellent option. Among other things, you may avoid potential problems when the resale value of the car is less than the residual value at the end of the lease. Leasing also entails fixed monthly payments over the term of the lease, which may be better if you are a small business owner. In addition, leasing may be preferable if you don't put many miles on your vehicle each year, since many current leases allow 12,000 or fewer miles each year.

Most people do not need to trade in their vehicles as frequently as manufacturers wish, so purchasing a vehicle and keeping it for a longer period of time typically yields much greater financial benefits. If you can pay for a vehicle within four or five years, the cost of driving it for five or six more years is often minimal, even if you have an occasional maintenance problem.

The bottom line: The best vehicle for you to drive may be the one you already have, especially if you already own it.

Purchasing Your Next Vehicle for Cash

How would you like to purchase your next vehicle for cash? Let me give you a workable strategy to do what many consider "impossible."

Let's assume we can purchase a new SUV for $25,000, and after five years the resale value would be $7,000. Purchasing the SUV over five years at a 10 percent interest rate would give us monthly payments of $488.68. Over five years our total payments would be $29,321 ($488.68 x 60 months). If we subtract the resale value of $7,000, the cost of the SUV itself (not counting gas, insurance, and maintenance costs) would be $22,321.

If we purchase a $10,000 used car, however, our monthly payments would be only $169.97. If we made the same payments we would have made on the SUV, we could pay off this used vehicle in 18 months. During the remaining three-and-a-half years we could put the same monthly payments into an investment that yields the same rate of return as the interest we were paying and have $24,703 in our investment account at the end of five years.

Admittedly, the cheaper used car would not be seen as an indicator of your success, nor would it be highly impressive in your office parking lot. It would, however, be far more attractive financially.

First, the cost of the SUV versus that of the cheaper car is actually $47,024 ($22,321 outflow versus an inflow of $24,703).

Second, by not buying the SUV now you'll be able to purchase the same vehicle five years from now for cash!

Can you imagine how great it would feel to be able to walk into a dealership and pay for your next vehicle in cash? However, if you do this, don't be surprised, as I once was, when the salesperson could only quote the monthly cost and not the outright purchase price.

Your being able to pay for a vehicle with cash will surprise everyone. It also may give you some additional leverage as you negotiate the actual sale price.

The Lottery/Gambling Trap

In the U.S. more money is now spent on gambling than on groceries. This is a sad commentary of the true state of our country, isn't it?

Most lottery advertising focuses on promoting the benefits to either schools or winners. For some reason they never showcase the tens of millions of losers. In consequence, more Americans are falling into the lottery trap every week.

Of course, no financial advisor in his right mind would endorse gambling. So what's the faulty thinking behind playing the lottery and other forms of gambling?

First, people believe that because *someone* is going to win big, that someone might be them (as long as they continue to play). Fact: you have a better chance of being struck by lightning than of winning the lottery.

Second, people believe that if they win big they'll stop gambling and live it up. Fact: people who win small amounts become addicted to gambling and can't stop. According to experts in Las Vegas, if you keep playing the house eventually always wins.

Third, people believe they can afford to gamble. Fact: in doing so most people waste a large chunk of the money they could have used to retire at age 67 or even earlier.

Fourth, people believe they'll be rich once they win big. Fact: research studies have proved that most winners are bankrupt within a few short years of winning millions because these individuals have already proven their inability to handle money.

So far I have met three major lottery winners. Two were almost completely broke within four years of winning. The third person managed to do well by getting appropriate legal and investment advice and investing the funds appropriately.

Many individuals could become millionaires by investing their funds instead of gambling them away over 15, 20, or 30 years.

PRACTICAL EXAMPLE

If a person stopped gambling and invested $60 a week for 35 years (at a 10 percent return), he or she would end up with a million dollars. If the same person invested $120 a week they would have a million dollars in 20 years. If he invested $240 a week, he would be a millionaire in only 15 years. Imagine!

People who play the lottery typically live within the lower levels of our economic system. Regardless of one's economic status, the lottery is a voluntary tax. Why pay it?

Again, society and advertising downplay the facts and wrongly claim that we can all be winners! Sadly, there need to be tens of millions of losers for the system to work.

America is still the land of opportunity. Interestingly, new immigrants to this country have rates of entrepreneurial success that are twice as high as those of citizens who have lived here for years or all of their lives. Let's never forget that there are wonderful opportunities for advancement in this country, regardless of who we are.

We live in a great country, we should be grateful for the opportunities we enjoy, and we need to make sure we don't let gambling and other poor choices wreak havoc in our lives.

Co-Signing for Someone Else

Before we wrap up this chapter, I want to take a few minutes to address what appears to be the most innocuous or improbable budget buster. This buster is co-signing someone else's loan. Co-signing means that you are agreeing to take over payment of someone else's loan the minute they stop doing so.

Remember that banks and other companies that loan money are experts. If they have looked at the evidence and determined that the individual or couple is a substantive credit risk, with a high probability of defaulting on the loan within a year or two (while still enjoying the goods or services rendered), who are we to question their judgment?

Ask anyone in the world of lending. A large majority of the individuals and couples who co-sign loans end up paying those loans. And their reward? Lost money. Guilt. Shame. Anger. Bitterness.

True, there may come a time when you feel it's necessary to co-sign a loan for a young adult child or extended family member. But don't forget that countless family relationships have been destroyed, and marriages dissolved, over this issue.

In such situations, (1) know in detail what you are guaranteeing to pay (in the event of default on the part of the principal party involved in the purchase), (2) put all of that money in a savings account in case you find yourself needing to pay off the loan, and (3) treat the money as a future gift to that family member. It's highly probable that you'll have to pay for the loan, so (4) don't act surprised, shocked, or disappointed when that becomes a reality.

If you are ever asked to co-sign, simply say, "I'm sorry, but I can't!"

Making the Commitment to Change

When it comes to personal finances, we all have the ability to make necessary life changes, but often we don't have the corresponding desire to change.

The commitment to change today rests with you! Do you have this desire?

The only way you will be able to transform your finances is to have both the desire and the commitment to change.

If you are married, both spouses must have this desire and commitment. Of course, we often marry a very different person from who we are, with differing desires, levels of commitment, and perceptions of the importance of accountability. Remember that the changes you two are making are for the good of both of you (or you individually, if you are single)!

Are You Feeling Wealthy?

So, how are you feeling after everything we covered in this session? Wealthy? Or poor?

To begin to put your current financial situation into perspective, 20 percent of the world's population earns less than $1 per day. Another 20 percent earns less than $2 per day. On the opposite end of the financial spectrum, only 20 percent of the world's population earns more than $70 per day, $490 per week, or $25,480 per year.

Most likely you are among the top 20 percent of income earners in the world today.

Employee Benefits

I am sure you have or will soon experience both the benefits and the confusion often provided by our employers' human resource departments. While all of the detail make sense to them, as they have worked with these benefits for many years, it can be confusing at best for the workers. For example, in terms of health care you may be given the choice of either a high-deductible plan with an HSA component or a more traditional option, with payments made by you, the employee, and deducted each month from your paychecks. This section will provide some guidelines for you to think about.

Health Care Benefits

Ordinarily there are not many options when it comes to health insurance today. The choice will typically come down to either a high deductible or a traditional plan. Unfortunately, one is not normally better than the other . . . they are just different. In my case I am offered two different types of health care plans: the first type I need to pay the first $6,000 in medical expenses (high deductible plan) and have the option of utilizing an HSA to pay for those expenses. I also have the option of a more traditional plan which covers the expenses sooner, but I end up paying $500 per month, which is deducted from my check. Based on this amounts, if I choose the option where I have a high deductible, I try to stack all of my medical expenses in one year. Therefore, there is an opportunity to pay less annually than the $500 fixed amount with the traditional plan. In addition, with the HSA option, I have the opportunity to bank some of these medical funds for future years if I don't spend them. In my case I feel the HSA is a better overall option. For someone else, the traditional health care plan may be preferable.

In general, health care plans are divided into two categories: HMO or PPO. With HMO the doctors are paid a fixed amount each year, regardless of whether or not you visit them. The objective of an HMO is that if the doctors keep their patients well, their waiting rooms will be less crowded with sick people. With a PPO the doctor is paid for each service rendered. One is not necessarily better than the other, and in most cases staying within the group of doctors you have provides the highest level of benefits at the lowest cost to you.

If your company is smaller and you are not provided health care benefits, your only real option is going to the Health Exchanges that exist within each state. The Affordable Care Act (Obamacare) has made significant changes to healthcare over the past few years and will continue to be significant for many people in the future. While there are still options today, I believe that at some point in your lives our country will adopt a single payer model. While we could spend all day debating the benefits or disadvantages of such a system, based on current political will and desire for control I predict that this will ultimately become a reality.

Dental/Vision

Dental and vision are other categories of insurance that are often offered by an employer. In both cases the employer may make a minimal contribution, but most of these costs are borne by the employee, who can choose whether coverage would be beneficial for them. In most cases today, dental insurance is provided by Delta Dental. Delta will pay 100% for routine examinations and split the costs 80/20 (Delta paying the 80%) for any additional work that is needed.

Vision is normally offered through insurance providers such as VSP and includes an eye exam and one pair of glasses each year. While these benefits are important if you wear glasses or contacts, they may not provide much benefit if you have excellent eyesight. This is one area in which you can weigh the costs against the associated benefits. Normally vision benefits are paid primarily by the employee but cost only a few dollars each pay period.

Disability Benefits

This is a benefit that may or may not be offered by your company. However, it is one that you should ask about. While the chances of your dying on the job are relatively slim, you have a one in three chance of becoming disabled during your career. This could either be for a short period of time or permanently. Most often these benefits are provided by your company. Again, it is good to ask about them when you are enrolling.

Life Insurance

Normally most firms offer 100% of your income as an automatic life insurance benefit. If the insurance provided is term insurance, the cost of the first $50,000 in life insurance is a non-taxed benefit. For amounts over $50,000 the cost of the life insurance will be added to your wages and included on your W-2. If your company offers whole life (rarely the case), the entire cost of the insurance is added to your wages.

In addition to the amounts that are automatically provided, most firms offer you the ability to purchase additional amounts at "group prices." While it is normally a good option to utilize this additional benefit, you need to make sure that any insurance purchased be portable after you leave the firm. I have witnessed a number of instances in which someone becomes sick, quits, and then dies. If the insurance cannot be carried outside the firm, the insurance will not be available when it is needed. If it is not portable, it most likely would be better to purchase this insurance outside your company, even though it may cost a few more dollars each month.

Retirement Benefits

Most firms today offer some form of retirement benefits. Usually this is a 401(k) plan; this designation simply refers to an IRS tax code section. All of these types of accounts will be listed later in this course.

The most important—as well as perhaps the most daunting—aspect of signing up for these types of plans is the investment selection process. Often this becomes so overwhelming that people simply don't sign up. In this case the government provides for an automatic signup with a 3% minimum contribution invested in lifestyle funds. In some firms I have seen 3 investment options, while in others there are over 100 funds that can be used. We will talk about investments later in this course, but one of the main things to remember is that the fund that performed well last year will very likely not be the highest performer this year. You need to pick investments that will provide an overall balanced portfolio for the future.

There are two types of tax options for many plans today. Most plans offer a traditional option, whereby contributions you make are not included in your wages and are therefore not immediately considered as income for tax purposes (you will still pay Social Security and Medicare taxes on all of your wages). Newer plan design allows for a ROTH type option, whereby there is no tax benefit today but you will also not have to pay any tax in the future when these funds are withdrawn. Just as with a ROTH IRA, if you are younger and at a relatively low-income level, this option will provide significant benefits.

There are a couple of important points to remember: (1) make sure that you contribute the maximum that will be matched by your employer. If you are matched 100% on the first 3%, make sure that you contribute at that level. If you are matched 50% on the first 5%, make sure that you are contributing accordingly; and (2) when you contribute 3%, your check will not go down by 3% because of the tax advantages of these types of plans.

Employee benefits are a significant part of everyone's overall financial planning. It is important to determine the benefits, as well as the gaps these benefits provide Worksheet 18 included in the back of this book will help you organize this information and lead you to ask good questions when you meet with your human resource department.

SESSION 4

EFFECTIVE INVESTING

Many people do not invest their monies effectively because they do not understand the various financial markets. Each day we hear about the gains or losses in the Dow Jones Industrial Average (DJIA), the Standard and Poor's 500, and the NASDAQ. We wonder how this translates into the value of our retirement plan or investments. In this section we will review the various financial markets to help us understand how they work and how we can use them to help us achieve our life goals.

Understanding Investment Options

Investments in today's financial world are becoming more and more complex. Also, the wide array of products offered by hundreds of financial institutions can become very confusing if we're not careful.

In most cases, investment products are not designed to be confusing. But all the features added to and offered with these products today (largely in response to customer requirements and needs) can quickly overwhelm the new investor. Add the necessary components of proper investment portfolio construction, and eyes tend to glaze over . . . just as yours are doing now! To allow you to better understand some of the available options, however, I want to give you a fairly simple framework you can use from here on out.

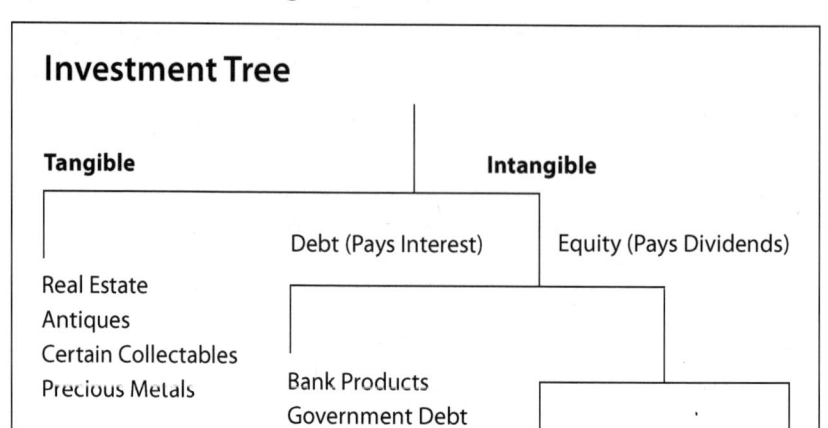

Tangible Versus Intangible Investments

Investment Tree

- **Tangible**
  - Real Estate
  - Antiques
  - Certain Collectables
  - Precious Metals
- **Intangible**
  - Debt (Pays Interest)
    - Bank Products
    - Government Debt
    - Corporate Debt
  - Equity (Pays Dividends)
    - Preferred Stock
    - Common Stock

As you look at the investment tree above you will see that it differentiates between tangible and intangible investments. Tangible investments are investments you can touch and feel, and you can often see their value. Investments in this category include homes, other real estate, certain antiques and collectables, and precious metals such as gold and platinum.

Although you might guess that automobiles would fall into this category, they don't because they virtually always depreciate in value over time (unless they're collectables).

Another tangible investment includes Real Estate Investment Trusts (REITS), which act like mutual funds but invest in shopping malls, office buildings, retirement complexes, and other forms of real estate. Although these investments are not often included in a portfolio, they offer an additional dimension that should be considered.

In his best-selling book *Rich Dad . . . Poor Dad*, Robert Kiyosaki noted that 97 percent of self-made millionaires became millionaires through real estate. If you look at that statistic alone, I believe you will agree that investments in real estate should be considered in any portfolio.

On the right side of the investment tree, we see various types of intangible investments. They are called intangible investments because we cannot touch or feel the value the security holds. Take a $1 bill from your wallet or purse and look at it. How much is this $1 bill worth? (This is not a trick question.) It's worth a dollar, of course. If I pay someone with a $1 bill, I receive a dollar's worth of goods or services in return.

Now look at this page closely. Can you tell me the difference between the paper used for this page and that used in the $1 bill? You might say that the paper used in the $1 bill is of higher quality and that it is therefore worth more than this page. Okay, then take a $20 bill out of your wallet and tell me the difference in value between the $1 and the $20 bill. I think you get the point!

The dollar bill is a piece of paper that has value because of who printed on it and what they printed, and because of those factors you will accept it as payment. Throughout history many things have been used as currency (the equivalent of money), including metals, spices, shells, sand, rocks, massive carved stones, and even tulip bulbs. All someone needs is an accepted medium of exchange for the payment process to occur.

Debt Investments

Intangible investments come in the form of debt or equity. Simply stated, any debt investment is a loan to someone else for a period of time. The return you receive for making this investment is interest.

One of the easiest ways to understand this type of investment is your home or car payments in reverse. Someone loaned you money that you used to purchase your home or car, and each month you are paying back part of the principal and all of that month's interest to that individual or entity. Of course, there are a number of types of debt instruments.

First, any type of bank product is a debt investment. When you put money into a checking or savings account or CD, you are loaning this money to the bank for a period of time. For the privilege of having this money to loan out to others, the bank often agrees to pay you interest in return, although typically a very small amount.

Second, any type of government note, bill, or bond is a loan to the government, and the "investor" receives a specific amount of interest over time. Most U.S. government investments today are considered safe because there is such a small risk of default (because the government can always print more money if necessary). Because these investments have so little risk, they don't earn a lot of interest over time. Subsequently, very few people invest in government bonds, but the government still needs to borrow funds. So a lot of U.S. bonds are sold to foreign countries, which may cause some huge problems in the future.

The third type of debt investment is loaning money to municipalities. Many cities borrow money to cover part of their budget or to finance convention centers, sports venues, and other large community projects. Often these municipal or "muni" bonds offer tax-free returns on both the state and federal levels. As a result, interest rates tend to be relatively low. Still, they're an investment worth actively considering.

Should someone consider investing in municipal bonds, though, specifically to avoid paying higher income taxes? The answer depends on the individual's marginal income tax rate (the amount of tax on the next dollar of earnings).

Let's look at the results for individuals in the 15, 28, and 35 percent federal tax brackets. We will assume that the interest rate of a corporate bond is 5 percent and the return on the municipal bond is only 3 percent. We will also assume a 5 percent state income tax. Here's what would happen if someone purchased a $1,000 corporate bond within each federal tax bracket:

	35 percent	28 percent	15 percent
Corporate bond interest	$50.00	$50.00	$50.00
Federal income tax	$17.50	$14.00	$ 7.50
State Income tax	$ 2.50	$ 2.50	$ 2.50
Total tax	$20.00	$16.50	$10.00
After-tax gain	$30.00	$33.50	$40.00
Municipal bond interest	$30.00	$30.00	$30.00
Difference	**$ 0.00**	**$ 3.50**	**$10.00**

As you can see, most individuals can get a higher return by purchasing a corporate bond and paying the required income taxes. Municipal bonds are generally beneficial only for those in the highest income tax bracket.

The fourth type of debt investment is loaning money to corporations. Many corporate entities borrow money on a regular basis to finance short-term seasonal or cyclical needs or long-term needs for capital projects or equipment (including production lines, airplanes, or ships).

In order to understand these investments better, some definitions may be helpful:

- **Maturity date:** The date on which, if you make the loan, you would get your money back.

- **Coupon rate:** The rate of return you would receive on your investment. For example, if the rate were 5 percent you would receive $50 per year for every $1,000 you invested.

- **Yield to maturity:** The actual return you would receive on your investment if you held the bond until maturity.

- **Bond risks:** The risk that you will not receive your initial investment amount (principal) back in the event of a corporate default or bankruptcy. For example, investors in companies like Enron, General Motors, or WorldCom a few years ago probably received a fairly high rate of interest, but they also faced a higher risk of not getting their money back. (I want to emphasize again that it is not the return *on* the investment that is most important but the return *of* the investment!)

- **Bond provisions:** There are a number of provisions that can be, and often are, included with the purchase of a bond. These are call and conversion provisions, which will be defined more fully below.

- **Call privileges:** These are an important consideration for investors for a number of reasons. Call provisions are rights given to the issuer (loaner) that allow him to pay back the loan at various times specified in the agreement. This may sound appealing to the issuer, but you as the loaner may get your money back when interest rates are low, causing you to purchase a new investment at a much higher level of risk in order to get the same amount of return. This is called reinvestment risk. If the loaner has this privilege, the loaner will pay a higher rate of interest.

- **Bond conversions:** This allows the loaner (corporation) to convert bonds for stock based on the details of the original loan agreement. This may protect the loaner from the stock going up rapidly or the quality of the bond deteriorating.

A company may also do this to ensure that its bonds are sold and generally will pay a higher rate of interest.

Some debt investments, including bank products, are stable. The value of others, including longer-term government and corporate bonds, can change based on the relative health of the economy, the strengths and weaknesses of the company, and interest rate fluctuations.

Some individuals try to gauge interest rate fluctuations in an attempt to profit from them. When Alan Greenspan was chairman of the Federal Reserve Board, some investors would look at how he was holding his briefcase on the day the Federal Reserve was scheduled to announce rates changes. Some claimed that if he was holding his briefcase with all five fingers it was heavy, which meant that the Federal Reserve was going to do something with the rates. If he held his briefcase with only two fingers, investors surmised that there would be no change and that the markets would trade normally. This may sound ridiculous, but investors regularly attempt to profit from such hunches.

The final type of debt investment we can make is in foreign governments or foreign corporations. While the interest rate returns on this type of investment are often appealing, there are additional risks. Those include political issues, currency fluctuations, and other factors that must be taken into account.

If you were able to get a 14 percent return on a New Zealand bond, yet the American dollar strengthened against the New Zealand dollar by 18 percent, the return would be negative 4 percent. Then again, if the American dollar were to weaken, the return could be huge.

Now we turn from one form of intangible investments to another.

Equity Investments

On the investment tree above, you see both preferred stocks and common stocks included on the equity side. Equity investments represent the ownership we have in a company. As an owner we do not receive interest on our investment. Instead, our return is paid in the form of dividends.

Preferred stock is considered a hybrid security since it contains many of the components of bonds, including a stated dividend rate and maturity. Preferred stock gets its name from being paid before the owners of common stock for dividends or company proceeds should the company go into bankruptcy. There is usually less volatility in the prices of preferred stock, even though it is an equity investment and there is no guarantee the investor will receive a dividend.

A number of provisions can be added to preferred stock. One is being callable like some debt investments. Other provisions can include being paid before any dividends are paid to shareholders of common stock and allowing preferred stockholders to receive additional earnings in times of significant corporate earnings (instead of common shareholders receiving all of the benefits).

Simply stated, common stock is straight ownership in a company. A few years ago one brokerage firm ran an advertisement featuring a kid showing up for baseball practice and telling his coach that his dad owns Nike. The coach has a vision of all of the kids in brand-new uniforms in a new stadium, all sporting the Nike logo. A few seconds later, the dad shows up with ketchup dripping down his Nike T-shirt, which notes his name and 0.00000000001 percent ownership of Nike.

This ad tried to prove a point. It was also an exceptional example of what company ownership is. If you were to purchase 500 shares of stock in a company like Nike, and there were 500 million total company shares, you would own a millionth of the company—and have a right to one millionth of the company's profits. You may not be able to say you own all of the door hinges or the sign in front of Nike's international headquarters in Beaverton, Oregon. Instead, you would own a very small faction of the entire company.

Common stock offers no guarantee that you will receive a return of your investment, let alone a dividend. Because common stock carries more risks than preferred stock, it often produces a higher level of return than other types of investments. It sometimes produces great losses, as well.

As with debt investments, you also have the option of investing in foreign markets, which does not necessarily mean investing in foreign companies. Just because a company is based in the United States doesn't mean its primary markets are here. Many firms have a significant foreign presence, and much of their planned growth over the next few years will come from their international operations.

Primary vs. Secondary Markets

There are two types of equity markets today: primary and secondary. When a company needs to raise funds for growth it will go first to the primary markets. Most of us know this market better as the initial public offering or (IPO) market. When a company decides to go public, it goes to large investment houses, which help it promote and sell its stock to individual investors. For example, a few years ago the software developer Google wanted to transition from a private to a public company. Through the primary market process, it created and sold its stock to individual investors. Google made a lot of money when the stock went public, and the individual investors have consequently also done well.

Once the stock is in the hands of individual investors, it will trade among investors on one or more secondary markets. Secondary markets can be categorized by how they conduct their trades—as either auction or negotiated. In the auction market system, there are individuals who will go to where the stock they are wishing to sell is being traded and look for another trader representing someone who wants to buy it. As there are often a number of buyers and sellers milling around an area where a particular stock is being traded, the scene can often get loud and interesting to watch; these traders compete for the best prices for both the seller and the buyer. Examples of an auction market include the New York Stock Exchange (NYSE); the American Stock Exchange (AMEX); and, if you are trading various commodities such as corn or wheat, the Chicago Board of Trade (CME Group).

The other type of secondary market is the negotiated market. Negotiated markets work like a giant eBay system of sorts in which traders can place offers to purchase or sell particular securities on a trading network, which allows all other traders to see the prices. Stocks can be purchased from the seller who is offering the best price and can be sold to the trader who is also offering the highest price. An interesting fact about this type of market is that it does not operate from a central location as auction markets do; rather, it is a giant computer network that provides the opportunities for investors to trade. One prime example of a negotiated market is the National Association of Securities Dealers Automated Quotation System, or, as it is better known, the NASDAQ.

Although the operations of the markets may differ based on the type of market system, the overall goals of the financial markets are the same: allowing individuals who own stock to sell to other individuals at a fair price in a competitive manner.

Knowledge of how financial markets work still does not answer the question of what happens when the DJIA (Dow Jones Industrial Average) rises and falls or what that really means in terms of your personal portfolio or 401(k). The DJIA is a fixed group of 30 stocks that are representative of many of the industry sectors in the United States. Individual stocks that are in this average are from many of the larger firms that have been around for many years, including IBM, American Express, Walmart, and General Motors. Periodically, stocks are switched to represent the current industry leaders of a particular sector. Walmart at one point replaced the retailer Woolworth, and Microsoft was added to the average to represent the technology sector. Each day the prices of these 30 move, and the change to the DJIA represents the change in price for these 30 stocks. (Note: For those of you who understand this better than most, you know that there is a factor that is also used as companies are added to or removed from the average, and that it is the price change multiplied by that factor that really creates the ups and downs with regard to the averages.) For the most part, with the exception of Microsoft all of the stocks on the DJIA are listed on the NYSE. Although many large companies, as well as a high percentage of the overall market, are traded on this exchange, there are other averages that better represent the overall financial markets. One of those is the Standard and Poor's 500, which represents 500 of the largest stocks and approximately 80 percent of the entire market valuation across all of the exchanges. Another is the NASDAQ Composite Index, which measures all NASDAQ domestic and non-U.S.-based common stocks listed on The NASDAQ Stock Market. This index is market-value weighted, which means that each company's security affects the Index in proportion to its market value. Those who want an even broader market exposure can look at the Wilshire 5000, which represents the performance of 5000 publicly traded stocks across all of the exchanges.

Generally, if the market indexes are positive for the day, the overall market has risen. However, there are a few instances in which the performance of one or two stocks in the average can move the average positively or negatively but not significantly impact the broader market index. Just because the average is higher does not mean that your stocks, or the value of your 401(k) portfolio, will also be.

When a stock goes public through the IPO process, the company offering the stock will choose the exchange on which it will trade. For some companies, the prestige and reputation of the NYSE will cause them to list on that exchange. Although there are some requirements for listing, such as the number of shares outstanding and the market capitalization, even relatively small firms have the option of listing on that exchange. Some companies in the technology industry, even though they are large and well respected, will choose to list on the NASDAQ because they want to be associated with an exchange that places a higher importance on the use of technology.

People usually use a symbol to represent the name of the company when they buy and sell equities. The symbol, which is selected by each company, consists of one or more characters that represent the name of the company. For example, Cedar Point Amusement uses the symbol FUN, and Brinker International, which owns a number of restaurant chains, uses EAT. If the company has three or fewer characters in its symbol, it will generally trade on one of the auction markets. If there are four or more characters in the symbol (Microsoft, for example, uses MSFT) it will generally trade on one of the negotiated markets. It is important to note that the financial markets in the United States have a very good reputation for service and fairness and are respected throughout the world. Many people throughout the world use our financial markets for their investments regardless of where they live because of this excellent reputation. One type of U.S. financial market is not necessarily better than another. They just operate differently. With the continued proliferation of technology, all of the financial markets are making greater use of technology to provide improved execution and service to their clients. Although some stocks on the auction market are traded on the floor of the exchange, an increasing amount of technology is used for trading smaller numbers of shares through various exchange computer systems. Although many people believe that auction markets are a dinosaur and will eventually be moved to a negotiated system, in reality the auction markets have used technology to execute an ever-increasing number of trades.

Understanding the Time Value of Money

One of the most foundational principles of finance is the time value of money.

We all know that money invested over time grows, not only from the interest you receive but also based on the compounding of the interest you have already received.

The time value of money can be seen in other ways, too. Which would you rather have: $20 today or $20 twenty years from now? I'm pretty sure you would choose $20 today, and you would be making the correct choice.

A number of problems are listed in this section to serve as an example of how the principle of the time value of money applies to our finances and the achievement of our goals. The calculations in this section can be performed easily using a calculator that has financial functions (one of them is the TI-83, which is what most teenagers use in school). If you do not have access to this calculator, you can find financial calculators in office supply stores, use functions in Microsoft Excel, or use any of a number of online websites that allow individuals to perform financial calculations.

Here are some sample problems with solutions:

1. How much would you have if you invested $10,000 today, left it in an account for 40 years, and earned 10 percent interest? The answer to this problem is $452,592.26. That is a very large sum of money accumulated in four decades. In a different example, how much money would you have if you used the $10,000 to purchase a car? After far fewer than 40 years of use the car would be worth nearly $0.

2. Will the difference of a few percentage points in the interest return you receive make that much of a difference? Let's say that you have $10,000 today and invest it at 2, 4, 6, 8, 10, or 12 percent interest. Here are the amounts you would have in 35 years:

2 percent return	$19,998.90
4 percent return	$39,460.89
6 percent return	$76,860.87
8 percent return	$147,853.33
10 percent return	$281,024.37
12 percent return	$527,996.20

As you can see, there is a significant difference in the amounts you would end up with. It is important to remember that these differences don't require *you* to work any harder; rather, your money is working harder for you.

As you also will note, to get the higher returns you probably won't keep your money in a bank or in lower risk investments. Instead, you'll need to invest in things that provide a higher return. To get higher returns, you have to be willing to incur a correspondingly higher risk.

3. What if every year for the next 35 years you would have another $4,000 to invest? Here is how much you would have at the end of the 35 years:

2 percent return	$203,977.47
4 percent return	$306,393.26
6 percent return	$472,483.47
8 percent return	$744,408.59
10 percent return	$1,192,507.22
12 percent return	$1,933,852.46

   A small amount of money invested appropriately on a regular basis can provide significant returns in the future.

4. If you want to start a business in 20 years at a startup cost of $50,000, you could either deposit $8,320.64 as a lump sum today or $74.31 per month in order to meet this goal, assuming you could obtain a 9 percent investment return.

5. I like to joke that there is only one thing worse than dying, and that is to outlive your money. Let's assume you are 40 years old, you want to retire at age 60, and you hope to live to 95 years of age. Although this may seem like a particularly long lifespan, with all of the advances in modern medical technology it's a more likely lifespan than most people realize. Then again, if I'm wrong, you'll die with plenty of money.

Let's assume you want to set aside the equivalent $50,000 per year in today's dollars for retirement. If you earn 8 percent on your investments, but inflation runs 3.5 percent, the amount you'll need to have saved by retirement is $1,849,391.27.

If you started at age 20 to meet this goal you would need to save $1,047.13 per month. At age 30 the amount would be $1,738.82. If your current age is 40, however, the amount is $3,118.98, and if you wait until you are 50 years old the amount will be a whopping $7,118.96 per month.

You may be thinking *Where am I going to get that kind of money from my current budget?* There is no easy answer. We simply have to choose what it is we will do without today in order to have what we will need in the future.

The time value of money also can be used to determine the true costs of some of our habits. Let's assume a potential return of 10 percent on your money. If you drink $4.50 worth of coffee daily at Starbucks for your entire working career, you've lost $626,848.29 in retirement funds. If you smoke one $5.00 pack of cigarettes a day, the cost over 40 years is $977,888.35. If you purchase lottery tickets at a rate of $50 per week, you've forfeited the opportunity to be a millionaire in well under 40 years.

Life is full of choices, and the money we spend today may limit some of our choices in the future. The reverse is also true. You can make very small daily sacrifices and still reap huge rewards when you reach retirement age. Also, just think about the immense amount of time you'll save not standing in line all the time.

Understanding Your Personal Risk Tolerance

Before making any investments, it is important that you take the time to assess your personal risk tolerance. In addition, if you are married you need to assess the personal risk tolerance of your spouse. During all of my years of managing investments for couples, I have never encountered a husband and wife who shared the same level of risk tolerance. Instead, I have often commented how funny it is that two individuals frequently end up together who are almost polar opposites with respect to their risk tolerances.

Before we go any further, how would you describe your risk tolerance? If the stock market were to decline by 40 percent tomorrow, what would be your reaction? Would you say that now is one of the best times to invest? Would you sell everything to get out of the market? Or would you simply hold on to what you have and not invest any more?

Each of these options describes a different tolerance for risk. Some individuals tend to be very aggressive and take considerable risks in order to potentially receive greater returns on their money. Some others are very conservative. For them investing in the stock market is perceived as too risky, and they feel much safer leaving their assets in banks or government investments. Neither approach is wrong.

Knowing your personal risk tolerance is important for two reasons. First, it will present you from making investments that will pose risks that exceed your tolerance. I am a firm believer that greater investment returns are not worth daily worry and sleepless nights. You have to choose what's right for you. Second, knowing your risk tolerance can increase your returns by allowing you to use asset allocation models, which I'll explain later.

To determine your risk tolerance, you need to ask yourself the following question: *How much loss in the value of my investments would cause me concern at this stage of my life?*

If you are older with minimal savings, you may not have any tolerance for risk and would be concerned if you lost any of the value of your investments. If you are younger, with many years of work ahead of you, you may be willing to take on greater risks in the hope of realizing greater returns.

With today's relatively volatile interest rates, individuals on a fixed income often take greater risks to maintain the same level of income. Although that may seem like an effective investment strategy, they also need to be concerned about the quality of their investments. Remember that these days it is not the return on the investment that's important; rather, it is the return *of* the investment that is critical! It is useless to have a 20 percent annual return on your investment, only to run the risk of losing everything six years from now. Always heed this sound advice from the investment guru Warren Buffett of Berkshire Hathaway:

> **Rule #1. Don't lose money.**
> **Rule #2. Don't forget Rule #1.**

Your First Investment

One of the questions I am often asked is "What is the best investment I should make at this point?" After much thought, I finally arrived at the world's most perfect investment. Here are some of the characteristics of this investment:

- fits into virtually anyone's personal risk tolerance
- has an incredible guaranteed return of between 13 and 30 percent per year
- is an investment anyone can make (without the help of investment brokers, financial advisors, or other professionals)
- works with an investment of any amount in a given month (even $5 makes a difference)

Interested in this investment? I hope so! All you need to do is start paying off your credit cards. With the average U.S. household carrying up to $9,000 in credit card debt, your best investment is paying off that debt. The return you will receive over time will be substantially higher than any other investment you can make.

Before you invest one dollar elsewhere, it's a must: pay off your credit cards!

Your Second Investment

After paying off your credit cards, the next investment you should make is to set up an emergency fund. Emergencies include losing your job or incurring huge medical bills.

Emergencies don't include replacing the roof of your house or repairing your car, which are ordinary expenses that should be anticipated and funded by the savings accounts you will set up within your budget.

How big should your emergency fund be? Ideally, it should cover all of your essential expenses for six months (once you factor in your state's unemployment benefits). That sounds like a lot, but the reality is that it could take more than half a year to find a new job.

Your initial goal for an emergency fund, though, should be enough to cover expenses for a month. Once you reach that level, focus on saving enough for three months. Then continue until you have six months covered.

Of course, the ultimate goal is up to you. The total you put into this emergency fund will depend in part on how long you want to be protected, the relative availability of jobs within your area, your preferred lifestyle, and your ability to change your lifestyle quickly should the need arise.

Where should these emergency funds be held? Options include money market accounts, savings accounts, or short-term bank CDs. The most important consideration is that your funds must be at no risk of being lost. The next consideration is some form of return, although if you use a savings account this return may be quite small. Even if the return is small, you want to make sure the funds will always be there in case of emergency.

Considering New Investment Options

Once you have your credit cards paid off and have established a sizeable emergency fund, it's time to move into the third stage of investing, which includes investing in financial securities. Before we proceed with these types of investments, it is important to gain some knowledge of the various investment options, the strategies currently used by investors for managing these invested funds, how the financial markets work, and the various types of accounts we can establish. This section focuses on these critical investment factors.

Separating Investment Vehicles from Investments

Often people are confused about investing because they don't understand the difference between actual investments and the vehicles or types of accounts used to make these investments.

We will first focus on the various types of investments we can make. For example, consider the following: Can you invest in stocks with an Individual Retirement Account (IRA)? Stocks can be purchased using a variety of account types. An IRA is one vehicle or type of account used to make such investments.

What are effective strategies for investments today? People are currently getting investment advice from everywhere and almost everyone. As we think about the advice we continually take in from the media, we recognize that it is both conflicting and confusing. There are a number of magazines sitting on news racks that make bold predictions about the future. However, we need to remember that these predictions are made more to sell magazines than to give appropriate advice—nor are the magazines responsible for the quality of the advice they give. There are also a number of television shows which features investment recommendations, which many people listen to, and follow their advice. The television personalities look like geniuses, but it is nothing more than a general reaction to the market based on investor demand. When you are confused about your 401(k) statement, do you just pick the funds that performed the best during the past year? Or seek advice from family members or friends, who often are just as confused as you are about the financial markets.

Society wants to bombard us with solutions for managing our funds, but by learning to understand investments we put ourselves in a much better position for investing these resources effectively. Regardless of the strategies used, successful investing comes down to one single point: time and not timing.

To help you better understand investment strategies, it is important to review some of them that are currently being used. These include active management, passive management, technical analysis, and marketing timing.

Active vs. Passive Investing

It is important to understand that a variety of investment styles currently exist, from the incredibly complex forms of technical analysis to the throwing of a dart at the dartboard to which has been affixed a *Wall Street Journal* stock page. Each of these methods has at times had limited success. It is also important to recognize that there is no one method that will always guarantee returns that will beat the overall market averages consistently. Therefore, we will begin looking at investment strategies by asking a simple but very important question: By making effective investments, can a person beat the overall returns of the market over time? Your answer to that question will determine what type of investment strategy you may prefer. A passive investment strategy holds that over time an investor generally cannot beat the market, so instead of trying to pick appropriate securities one just goes out and purchases all of the various securities within a certain market index or sector. For example, an investor who wishes to purchase a portfolio of general equity securities could purchase an S&P 500 index fund, which would purchase an interest in all 500 of the largest companies listed on all of the major exchanges. Purchasing this one asset would provide an investment into almost 80% of all of the publicly traded companies. If you wanted to purchase an investment that would give you greater exposure, you could purchase a fund like the Wilshire 5000, which invests in all 5,000 of the largest publicly traded companies. A passive strategy will yield the returns of the general market, either positive or negative. There are a number of firms that specialize in this approach, including the Vanguard Funds, which were among the first to utilize this strategy. More recently, due to the success and investor interest in this strategy, the various index- or exchange-traded funds are offered by a number of financial firms.

An active investment strategy holds that appropriate research and picking exceptional stocks will yield higher returns over time. There are many firms that utilize this strategy, including a number of mutual fund companies, such as the popular American Funds, and various insurance firms.

At this point I am sure you are wondering which of these strategies is best. The simple answer is it that it depends. One of the major differences between these two strategies is the associated internal investment management fees that are charged by the company managing the funds. There is usually minimal management expense with purchasing all stocks within various market indexes, which keeps the fees these funds charge very low. The average internal expenses of actively managed funds are approximately 1.45%; most of the passively managed funds charge below .5%, with many of the better ones charging below .2%. Lower expenses (which take less from your investment returns) are one way that a passive strategy can often beat an active strategy over time. Second, the tax efficiency of index funds can often delay the tax on investment gains. There are actively managed funds with good tax efficiency, but there are others that turn over their entire portfolio frequently, causing an individual to incur capital gains taxes with no investment returns (it is important to note that these taxes apply only to taxable accounts, not to retirement accounts like a 401k or an IRA).

Technical Analysis and Market Timing

Technical analysis and marketing timing are two other techniques that investors use to determine whether to buy or sell a particular security. Technical analysis is usually accomplished by sophisticated computer software, along with data feeds from a number of the financial markets to supply the software with the necessary trading information. Individuals who rely on technical analysis spend their time looking at the various stocks' trading patterns and transmit signals to traders who use this information to execute their buy and sell decisions. Technical analysis is often touted by infomercials or investment seminars as a way for common individuals to profit by using their software and systems. Often these infomercials are accompanied by glowing testimonials concerning the success of the system. Although the advice may sound valid, and there may be some historical support for these systems on a macro basis, many people spend thousands of dollars on systems only to find that they experience only periodic success. One of the questions I often ask individuals who buy these systems is this: If everyone were to use these types of systems, would this not neutralize their benefits for all who rely on them? Often we may think that through their use we gain some special, insider knowledge about a company whose stock we would like to buy or sell. In reality, however, the various news feeds and company announcements no longer offer much inside or non-public information about a company due to blogs and other forms of technology.

Market timing considers the economic cycles and makes trading decisions based on where the economy is in the current cycle. At the peak of an economic cycle, the point at which prices of stocks are at their highest, one would usually sell stocks, believing that their prices would likely decrease as the cycle changed. Buying at the bottom of an economic cycle is another strategy. However, one must ask how accurately one can really time the market. Based on my calculations, one would need to be absolutely, 100% right on the upside side of the scale, and 50% right on the downside, just to break even—this would be very difficult to accomplish.

A number of publications have presented the disadvantages of market timing. They note that by losing the best days over a period, such as ten years, your investment results will be dramatically lower than the averages over the same period of time. Although this may make for interesting reading, one needs to also look at the other side and ask what would happen if an investor would be out of the market during the worst days of that same period. One can easily see that there is greater benefit to being out of the market during the worst trading days than to being in on the best trading days during a ten-year period:

	Missing the Best	Missing the Worst
10 Days	14.24%	24.17%
20 Days	11.99%	27.04%
30 Days	10.01%	29.45%
40 Days	8.23%	31.66%

I hope you can see through this discussion that although all of the above investment methodologies may sound good, and can be used by individuals, there is no one system that guarantees positive returns. If there were such a system, everyone would be using it, or the person who developed it would not be sharing it with others but using it privately to increase her own wealth. Most providers of investment systems are simply in the business of selling the systems and providing training in how to use them.

One thing I have noticed over the years during which I have been investing is that one of the important measures of investment success is time. Although no one can predict what the market will do today or tomorrow, it is still generally true that if we invest over a longer period of time we will end up with a positive return.

Matching Investments with Available Time

I am confident that you formulated both your short- and long-term goals as you worked through previous sections of this book. When you make investments, it is important that the investment selected produces returns by the time needed to achieve your goal. An example of this is investing for your child's education. You may appropriately invest in the stock market using mutual funds while he is younger, but as the time for the use of these funds nears, the risk should go down. When the child is ready to use these funds, there should be no risk of losing principal, and an appropriate investment at this point will be in money market funds. On the other hand, many of you may believe that as you near retirement you should switch your investments in order to lower the risk to your principal. Although this may sound good in principle, I would suggest that it may be a questionable strategy. When you are 30 years old you can make a number of risky investments as you predict there will be many years of working ahead of you. When you turn 65, you also generally have many years of life still ahead of you. Although I do not believe you should risk all of the principal assets you have set aside for retirement, there are some assets you should invest for a 10- or 15-year timeframe, while keeping other assets invested appropriately in shorter-term investments for the next 10 years.

> ### PRACTICAL EXAMPLE
>
> *When you invest your funds into a 401(k) plan while you are working, it is generally recommended that you take significant risks while you are younger, as you will have sufficient time to recover if there are market declines, and you hope to reach your goal a number of years in the future. If you invest in a risky manner when you are older, you will not have the time you will need if market problems cause loss at this time. It is important to continually review the amount of time you have before you expect or need to realize your goals.*

What About Risk?

One of the most fundamental aspects of investing has to do with risk and return. Generally speaking, the more risk one takes in investing, the higher the level of the expected return. For example, when one invests in U.S. government treasury bills there will be very little return but also very little risk of the U.S. government defaulting on paying the interest or returning the principal. Small capitalization stocks or startup companies face a greater risk of going under than, for example, IBM or Apple. Therefore, the expected returns on small company stocks are generally higher than on those of larger companies.

There is really no way to eliminate risk when one invests. You may be saying that keeping your cash in a mattress at home has no risk, as it will not go down in value. However, what happens if your house burns down? In addition, inflation will cause the purchasing power of your cash to decline over time.

Risk is not one-dimensional, and often there are multiple risks to consider when investing. This section will provide some of the risks that you need to be aware of when you make an investment:

Inflation Risk — The risk of the purchasing power of your assets going down over time. With inflation, things generally will cost more in the future than they do today. If your investments do not keep up with inflation, your purchasing power will go down. When you keep your money "safe," oftentimes you will lose a portion of its purchasing power. To make sure you stay ahead of inflation, you need to purchase investments that are growing faster than the inflation rate.

Market Risk — The risk of the market rising or falling faster than anticipated. While we like it when markets rise—even rise quickly—we fear market declines. We need to understand that markets rise and fall on a regular basis and that we cannot predict the timing of these events.

Credit/Default Risk — When you purchase a bond there is a chance that the loaner will not be able to pay you back. The lender could be a company, municipality, or government entity. This likelihood can be determined by looking at the bond rating, which demonstrates the credit quality of the bond. The lower the bond rating, the higher the interest it will generally pay.

Interest Rate Risk — When interest rates rise, the prices of the bonds will fall. Conversely, when interest rates fall, bond prices will rise. When interest rates rise people tend to sell stocks and put the proceeds into debt instruments such as bank products. Over the past few years interest rates have been very low. As they will most likely rise in the future, the prices of bonds will tend to fall. Therefore, you most likely will not want to purchase a long-term bond.

Reinvestment Risk — If a bond is called early, you may have to reinvest these funds in bonds that pay a lower rate than what you received before.

Political/Legislative Risk — When changes are made to factors such as tax laws, this does have an effect on the overall markets. Some of these are positive changes; others can have a negative effect. In addition, on an international level changes in regimes or players affect markets on a global scale. Examples of this include Britain leaving the European Union and, more recently, changes in political structures in Italy and Cuba.

Exchange Rate Risk — When you invest internationally you most likely will need to bring these funds back to the United States. When this happens you most likely will most likely, due to the fluctuation in exchange rates, receive back a different amount than you withdrew at the time you moved the funds. Again, sometimes this difference is positive and sometimes negative.

Asset Allocation

The concept of asset allocation includes more than just putting all of your eggs into one basket or looking at a pie chart to see how your portfolio is being allocated. Rather, a true asset allocation model analysis consists of various asset categories in order to get the highest return for the risk you take. By combining specific asset categories using relatively sophisticated mathematical models, you will reduce the volatility of the returns.

Asset allocation will generally allow one to get higher returns by investing in many different classes of assets. This enables one to achieve higher returns while minimizing risks. An example of this would be an individual who is currently investing in bank CDs. By moving his investment to corporate bonds, he will incur relatively minimal additional risks, but the improved returns can often be substantial.

What is most interesting with regard to the concept of asset allocation is that in a study of major pension funds 93.6% of a portfolio's return was found to be a result of the asset allocation, with only a minor portion coming from the specific investment securities that were selected (Gibson, 1990). Only a minor performance improvement occurred based on the specific assets that were in the portfolio. Therefore, it is more important that we develop the correct asset allocation model within our portfolios than that we spend time determining whether we should invest in IBM or General Electric (both of which fall into the same asset class). Asset allocation is used today in a variety of settings, including lifestyle mutual funds, target mutual funds, and funds that are specifically called asset allocated funds.

Selecting Appropriate Securities

The securities selection process requires one basic decision: to hire it out or do it yourself? If you hire it out, you will need to select a competent advisor and give her the necessary time to allow her to help you through the financial planning process. Unfortunately, clients tend to move money between managers based on their relative performance that particular quarter or year. If you make the commitment to hire this out, you need to commit to working with this advisor over a period of time to see how the plan develops.

If one does it for himself, one needs to make the commitment to take the time to learn, to do his homework before investing, and to take the necessary time to track and manage the securities he has invested in. For some of you, this may sound like hard, time-consuming work—which it can be! One strategy investors can use to learn more about the investment selection process is to become a member of a local investment club. An investment club, often working through the National Association of Investment Clubs, can provide the tools, forms, and environment necessary for gaining critical knowledge of this area.

One question many individuals have when starting an investment program is whether they should seek out appropriate advice for their investment selections or do it alone. Most financial magazines and internet sources want us to believe that we can go it alone and that their publications are all we need for appropriate advice. In reality, even though we all have other unique abilities, most of us do not have investment experience. Even though we could invest our financial resources on our own, most of us would rather be doing other activities than taking the necessary time to manage our funds in a proper manner. By not taking the time required to learn various investment strategies, we will not be disciplined in our research and, typically, will invest based on the latest hot stock or on investment tips from family, coworkers, or friends. If you wish to go it alone, it is highly recommended that you join a local investment club sponsored by the NAIC, which provides a number of tools and resources to new or novice investors.

For most people it would be best to seek appropriate advice from a financial planner who has the expertise not only in investments but also in general financial and estate planning.

Effective Investing 125

Typically, this planner would enable you to get higher returns over time by forcing you to be disciplined in your investing and by having these investments be a part of a comprehensive program to meet your individual goals and objectives throughout the rest of your life. In the next section we will discuss the various professional financial designations and what their titles mean to you as your start your investment program.

Setting Up Your First Brokerage Account

There are a number of ways by which an individual investor can purchase securities today. This section will review a number of possible options, including dividend reinvestment programs, brokerage accounts, mutual funds, and annuities. After listing the various options, information will be given as to how to set up your first account.

Direct Purchase

Many corporations allow you to directly invest in the company and, once you have shares, to reinvest the dividends in the company. Depending on the program offered, dividend reinvestment programs or DRIPs allow investors to either take the dividends that would usually be paid to the investor and reinvest them in the company's stock or make periodic contributions and use them to purchase additional shares on a regular basis.

The advantage of this type of program is the low transaction costs of purchasing the stock based on the larger number of shares purchased at a time, and the costs of the accounts, which are usually paid for by the company. The disadvantages of a DRIP program are that you pay tax on the dividends you received (even though they are reinvested). You will also need to keep a record of all of these reinvested amounts so that when you sell the stock you can add the amounts of these dividends to the basic cost to prevent you from having to pay tax on the dividends twice (once when the dividend is paid, and again when the stock is sold in capital gains). If these records are not maintained, and the dividends are reinvested for many years, computing this can be a significant undertaking for the investor. To find out if a company offers this type of plan, an investor would usually go to the company's website and download the provisions that are offered.

Brokerage Accounts

A brokerage account is an account maintained at a brokerage firm through which individual securities can be purchased. There are a variety of full-service traditional firms, such as Merrill Lynch, or online firms, such as Fidelity, Schwab, E-Trade, or TD Ameritrade. There was a time when brokerage firms could add value to their trading abilities, and there were significant benefits associated with working with a specific brokerage firm. However, with the advent of the electronic age, actual transaction handling has become more of a commodity for most firms. When considering the various brokerage account options available, it is important to look beyond the actual costs to the provider who offers the best service and advice, based on your individual situation.

Another source to look at is the online service Robinhood. Robinhood allows you to make smaller dollar investments in fractional shares of stock at no cost (the cost is built into the execution price you are getting). While there may be better options for larger accounts, if you have enough money to purchase a ½ share of Apple, this system will allow you to do this in a cost-effective manner.

Mutual Funds

Thus far we have looked at purchasing individual securities. Although individual securities let individuals concentrate on a limited number of securities, most people would be better served by acquiring a variety of stocks or bonds in a simple investment. This requires a relatively small initial investment and allows the investor to make additional investments in a number of securities on a regular basis. For these reasons, mutual funds provide an effective and cost-efficient investment option. A mutual fund is nothing more than a pool of investor money that is invested in various securities. Each mutual fund has one or more investment managers who are responsible for managing the various funds and are paid for their services with internal fund expenses. Investments that are made by the fund are based on the fund's objectives. Investors can review the fund's objectives before they make their investment to ensure that the objectives match their specific risk tolerance and goals. Most mutual funds are included within a family of funds, offered by a fund provider who makes available a variety of funds with differing investment objectives. This allows individuals to move among various funds as their needs change, and also to invest in multiple funds to gain the advantage of differing fund objectives. One of the problems with mutual funds is that there is almost more variety in the number of mutual funds than there are individual securities, and selecting among the many funds is sometimes as difficult as selecting individual securities.

A significant benefit of a mutual fund is that it generally offers diversification. This lessens the chance of significant loss if one of the funds fails, as you still have a number of other securities that may do well. For example, if you had invested all of your money in Enron stock a few years ago, you would have lost all of it. However, if the mutual fund had invested only some of its portfolio in this company, although they would have lost this investment it would likely have been only a small part of their entire portfolio.

One of the questions concerning mutual funds that often arises is the difference between loaded and no-load funds. No-load funds do not have any up-front expense charges when a person purchases the securities. Loaded funds charge an additional fee to compensate the broker who sold the fund to you. When the no-load funds were introduced, many financial advisors isisted that they yielded lower returns than their loaded counterparts. This was quickly proved wrong. What advisors should have said was that no-load funds offer no advice. Although some believe that the performance of all funds is comparable, having someone to guide you through this investment maze, help you define your goals, and provide appropriate advice may be helpful in the long run and produce a higher investment return. Loaded funds are typically divided into share classes. Different rates of commission are charged based on the class and family of funds that are being managed. These fees would be in addition to the amount charged for fund management. Some of the most used share classes include:

- **A Share class:** These funds charge a front-end charge (5.75%) that is shared between the broker (broker would normally receive 5% of the 5.75%) and the fund company, who would get the remainder. Although this up-front expense may seem high, annual expenses with this share class tend to be lower than those of other share classes or no-load funds. On the positive side, this class of shares is generally the cheapest way to go if you have a longer time horizon with these investments. On the negative side, with your advisor getting so much of the return upfront there is relatively little incentive for him to service your account for many years into the future. Often, if you do not keep investing with this broker, you are transitioned out ("fired") so that the investment advisor will have more time to spend on accounts that are paying or have more revenue potential for the advisor.

- **B Share class:** With this share class you are not charged an initial expense but are charged an annual rate (usually an additional 1%) for a period of years after the investment is purchased. There are instances in which this additional expense may run for seven or more years. If you try to remove these investments before that time there will be a "back-end" charge to recoup the expenses that would have been charged if the investment had not been removed.

- **C Class Shares:** Class C shares of mutual funds have a level load or normally 1% annually. That means that for each year you participate in the fund you will pay an additional internal expense of 1% for all of the money you have in the fund. I have always liked this method, even though it costs more than other share classes. I believe that it is the fairest system, as it removes the initial profit motive for the broker, keeps the broker or financial representative fairly compensated for his or her work for you each year, and allows you to easily change fund families or brokers if either is not performing. The only way the broker earns more is to increase your account size, which also provides a benefit since everyone is focused on the long-term growth of the account.

- **R Class Shares:** This class of shares is often used for retirement plans. Normally these shares compensate the broker based on the various types of R shares used and the overall size of the plan assets.

It is important to remember that regardless of which types of mutual funds you purchase there will be additional expenses each year for the management of the investments in the fund. The average amount charged for the fund management is approximately 1.45% per year. You do not see this charge, but it is annually taken out of the portfolio's investment performance.

If you have a larger sum of money, such as is the case with a rollover investment from a retirement account, you can often get a discount on the charges if you stay within one family of funds, but the fund management fees will stay constant. There are many advantages to mutual funds that make them appropriate for most individual investors.

Annuities

Annuities are offered by a number of insurance companies and most often take one of two forms: fixed or variable. With a fixed annuity, an investor places his or her money into an annuity, which earns a fixed rate for a period of time. The investments used to back up a fixed rate annuity are generally invested in bonds, real estate, or other fixed return products, which have a lower return than other investments but less volatility. When the investor retires or otherwise needs the money, he has the option of "annuitizing" the account, with a guaranteed fixed amount to be returned to him each month. These monthly payments are based on a variety of options selected by the investor, including a fixed amount for the rest of your life, for a joint life, or over a life with a guaranteed number of years of payments. With each additional guarantee the monthly amount received will be less. Although an individual's lifespan is unknown, based on insurance company mortality tables the insurance company knows that there are as many people who will live for more than 100 years as there are those who will die in the relatively near future. That is what allows the insurance company to provide the guarantees it does.

When one purchases a variable annuity, a separate investment account is created, which one can invest in a variety of investment options. These options most often include mutual funds from a number of mutual fund families. The returns on a variable annuity can be higher than those of a fixed annuity, but there is no guarantee of performance. The ultimate returns of the annuity, realized when the investor retires, can be more or less based on the individual performance of the secondary account.

Inasmuch as annuities are insurance products, any gain in the annuity or separate account is tax deferred until the removal of funds from the account. This is a significant benefit to high wage earners who would like to defer this income to another time when their income may be less and/or their tax bracket lower. There is no maximum investment one can make in an annuity, so this can be a substantial benefit to higher wage earners.

Over the past few years there have been a number of provisions added to variable annuity contracts that make them more effective in certain situations. Some contracts provide a guaranteed return per year, indexing the returns to market returns, new account incentives, and significant death benefits. Some of these options can be of significant advantage to certain investors, but they tend to confuse the average investor. These options may provide significant benefits, but they come with associated and often excessive fees. Many recent articles in the financial literature have presented these fees in a negative light and have recommended that investors not purchase such contracts due to these fees. However, some of the guarantees they offer make them appropriate in certain situations.

Setting up a financial savings account is a relatively simple process. Depending on the type of investment you select, forms will be required from both you and the investment firm. Due to recent acts of terrorism and money laundering, the amount of information you will need to provide a company has grown dramatically. If you use a traditional investment firm, these forms will be given to you, along with instructions on how to complete them. If an online firm is used, necessary forms can be downloaded, printed, and completed by the investor. As original signatures are often necessary on these documents, returning them by mail will be necessary before you will be able to use the account. Once the account is established, you can begin trading.

Get-Rich-Quick Schemes

Finally, as I look at the covers of business and financial magazines and watch infomercials on television, it's apparent that a lot of people want to sell me something to make me rich. Some claim that we can make millions in just a few hours a month using their real estate techniques or make thousands every week by buying and selling stocks using their technical reports.

Most Americans realize that the people selling these products are the only ones getting rich, while those who buy their products often get farther and farther behind financially. Get-rich-quick schemes are just that—schemes to get their hands on your hard-earned money.

I probably have seen almost every possible scheme out there. These include many real estate programs, multi-level marketing opportunities, oil field investments, and investment trading systems using technical charting, options, and foreign currency. With all of these systems I have always asked myself *If this system* makes money so easily, why are they trying to sell it to me? Why wouldn't they want to keep it a secret or use it themselves to make untold millions?* Of course, every scheme has a few success stories. But what's the average person's experience? Money out, more money out, . . . and little or no money back. Their advice: work harder, work smarter, network more, spend more. After all, "your turn's next." It's a lie. There is no such thing as a get-rich-quick system. Only schemes. Am I saying that none of these systems works? No, but most of them require hard work—over many years—to learn the system well enough to profit from it. There are much better uses of your time and money, believe me.

How Can We Teach Children?

Children are truly one of life's special gifts, and although they bring times of frustration they also bring immense joy! One of the responsibilities we have as parents is to teach our children financial concepts, and that can begin at a very early age. Looking back at my own children, there have been many times over the years in which they have received money, including Christmases, birthdays, allowances, and times of begging for anything and everything in a toy store. As parents, we often let our children spend all the money they receive during these times. What I would like to recommend is that you begin a process of 50/50 thinking with them. With this system you would require your children to take 50% of the money to be invested in a savings or mutual fund account for the future, allowing them to spend the remaining 50% on whatever they want. With this system, you would create a balanced lifestyle for them at an early age and also enable them to invest funds for future use.

UGMA/UTMA Accounts

Accounts for minors are normally set up as either a Uniform Gifts to Minors Act (UGMA), which allows a way for a minor to have an account without the costly expenses of setting up a trust, or a Uniform Transfers to Minors Act (UTMA), which allows a minor to own additional types of investments, including real estate, fine art, and patents. The benefits of such accounts is that investment returns under a certain amount would be reported on the child's tax return, which usually has a considerably lower rate than the parents'. One of the disadvantages of these types of accounts is that the custodian controls the funds until the minor is 18 years of age for the UGMA accounts, or 21 years of age for the UTMA accounts (depending on the state). After that time ownership reverts to the child. Although that may not seem to be a problem for some, I have seen cases in which an 18-year-old takes the amounts in these accounts as a windfall and spends all of the proceeds as soon as they are available to him.

Coverdale IRA Accounts

One option for parents who wish to begin a savings program for their children's college education is the Coverdale IRA account. This plan allows parents to contribute up to a certain amount each year (currently $2,000) to an account for use when their children enter college. If these accounts are used for postsecondary college tuition, college fees, books and related supplies, equipment, and certain room and board expenses, all of the gains will be distributed tax-free.

Many of the provisions of the Coverdale plan may seem similar to those of the 529 plan, which is described next. There are, however, differences in the amounts that can be contributed, the available investments, and what the funds can be used for. With the Coverdale IRA the maximum annual contribution is much lower than with a 529. However, the investment options available are much greater. In addition, this account can be used for elementary education tuition, which could be a significant benefit for parents who opt for private education.

529 Accounts

Many of you have identified being able to provide for the education of your children as one of your major life goals. The cost of a college education has grown considerably over the past few years, with costs increasing at a greater rate than inflation. Even though there are a number of available prepaid options for college tuition, many people do not have the financial resources necessary to afford them. There are a number of excellent ways to save for these future educational costs, including the use of a 529 plan. A 529 plan is a state-specific plan that allows parents or grandparents to invest funds, both now and in the future, and allows these funds to grow and be used tax free to pay higher education expenses. Each state has its own plan, and parents and grandparents can opt to use the plans of states that offer the most flexible funding options or have a preferred investment manager. If you look at a number of personal finance magazines, including Kiplinger's or Money, you will often find ratings for these plans and statement of the benefits each provides. Generally, 529 plans fall into one of two types: prepaid tuition plans and college savings plans.

Although these plans may sound relatively complicated, in reality they are quite simple. To fund a 529 plan one needs to open an account with a financial provider. Once the account has been opened, additional amounts can be invested at any time. Investments in the plan will be placed in a pooled account based on the child's age, and if the funds are used for higher educational expenses all amounts can be withdrawn tax free. What makes these accounts so attractive, other than the tax benefits and the fact that most college expenses can be paid for in this way, is that they can also be used for different types of schooling, including trade classes or other personal or professional training classes. If the child does not pursue additional education, these funds can be transferred to other siblings or cousins of the beneficiaries. I have also seen cases in which, if the children do not attend college, these funds revert back to the owner (parents or grandparents), allowing them to go on a number of worldwide educational adventures.

If funding your child's education is one of your personal goals, one strategy you can use is to take all Christmas or other gift money and use it to fund one of these accounts. Based on time value of money principles, you may be surprised at how these small amounts of money will grow over time and how many benefits they will later provide your students.

Prepaid Accounts

Like the other accounts discussed previously, these types of plans are used for college. What differs with these plans is that you pay for college tuition now (usually for a state college), and then when the child is old enough they may use up these prepaid semesters. The advantages are that if college costs increase faster than expected you have locked in the costs by prepaying. The disadvantages of these types of programs are that they need to be used at the college selected—What happens if the child wants to go to a trade-related school or even a different college? In these instances a 529 may offer you more flexibility to either move the funds to different beneficiaries or select other options for their use.

Understanding Financial Designations

One of the confusing aspects of working with a financial advisor is the seemingly myriad financial designations that exist for these advisors. In the field of accounting, in order to be certified you would obtain your Certified Public Accountant (CPA) designation, which is granted by the individual states. The financial world is a very different situation, with more than 125 designations. Some require little more than a fee, while other, more substantial designations require a significant amount of time and effort to secure. However, it is difficult for the average investor to determine which of the designations are meaningful. This section discusses four of the major designations and their meanings:

1. **Certified Financial Planner (CFP®)** is a certification granted by the Certified Financial Planner Board of Standards after the individual has completed a prestudy program and successfully passed a 10-hour certification exam. In addition to earning this designation, individuals are required to complete 15 hours of continuing education per year to maintain their certification.

2. **Chartered Life Underwriter (CLU)** is a designation granted by the American College. Individuals who hold this designation generally have a higher level of knowledge in the areas of life insurance and other insurance products. To complete the requirements for this designation, one needs to complete five classes, along with passing appropriate examinations for each of them.

3. **Chartered Financial Consultant (ChFC)** is also a designation granted by the American College, and like the CFP the certificant focuses more on long-term, comprehensive financial planning. To gain this certification

an individual needs to complete eight classes and pass examinations when each class is completed.

4. **Chartered Financial Analyst (CFA)** is a designation granted by the CFA Institute after the applicant has taken a number of exams in the selection of investment securities. This designation demonstrates that the individual has specific knowledge in the appropriate selection of financial securities.

With each of these designations there is generally an ethical code of standards that must be agreed to by the person holding the designation, along with specific degrees and years of experience before this designation can be used. Using an advisor with this designation, though not guaranteeing a higher level of performance, may help you in that they will take a more comprehensive approach to financial and investment planning.

SESSION 5

INSURANCE, TAXATION, RETIREMENT, AND ESTATE PLANNING

*I have enough money to retire and live
comfortably for the rest of my life.
The problem is I have to die next week.*

—ANONYMOUS

Insurances

House Insurance

As with most insurance policies purchased today, individuals pay a small premium (loss) each month to avoid a major loss in the future. Insurance works by pooling the risks of a large number of people and spreading the potential for loss over all of them. For example, while there may be the possibility of hurricane damage in Florida, not all of the homes there will be damaged in a storm. Also, by pooling all of the states together, in reality only a small percentage of homes will be destroyed in any one year. While insurance companies do not know which homes will be affected, this number can be projected (actuarially) and spread over all the policyholders.

There are six different policy forms based on a specific type of property. These forms include:

1. **HO-2:** The broad form covers damage to dwellings, other structures, and personal property caused by named perils.

2. **HO-3:** The special form is open, covering almost any type of physical damage to dwellings. However, HO-3 does not provide open peril coverage for personal property (only for the named perils). The special form is a better choice for most homeowners and costs approximately 10–15% more than HO-2.

3. **HO-5:** The comprehensive form is similar to HO-3 but provides open-perils coverage on personal property and costs about 15% more than HO-3. The same coverage can be obtained with a special endorsement.

4. **HO-8:** This modified coverage form is designed for older homes whose replacement value significantly exceeds fair market value.

For renters:

5. **HO-4:** The tenant form. Similar to HO-2 (broad form coverage) for those who rent apartments, rooms, and houses.

6. **HO-6:** The unit owner's form is designed to cover the special needs of condominium and co-op owners.

Normally the perils named in a policy include fire, lightning, windstorm or hail, explosion, riot or civil commotion, aircraft accidents, vehicles colliding with dwellings, smoke, vandalism, theft, damage to building glass, volcanic eruptions, collapse of building from weight of snow and ice, and falling objects.

In addition to the insurance forms noted above you can also obtain endorsements for specific coverage for earthquakes, replacement costs, or mold. In all cases you need to make sure your policy would cover a minimum of 80% (100% is preferred) of the cost to replace the overall structure. In addition, you need to determine the appropriate level of coverage for the home's contents.

In addition to the coverage, you also need to determine the deductible you would be willing to pay if there were a loss. For example, you would pay more for a policy with a $250 deductible than you would for one with a $1,000 deductible. The deductible is the amount you would have to pay for a loss before any money would be paid by the insurance company.

While the chance of a complete loss of your home is relatively small, you still need to have insurance, especially if you have a loan for the home. In addition, I can say from personal experience that I am amazed at what a homeowner's policy can cover. For example, when I flew to Hawaii my luggage never arrived. My homeowner's insurance covered my loss above what the airline covered. I carry an additional endorsement that covers all of the electronics in my home for damage, breakage, and loss. The coverage is more comprehensive than, say, AppleCare at only about a quarter of the price.

Auto Insurance

Auto insurance is very similar to home insurance in that the costs of accidents are spread over a large number of policyholders. As with home insurance, the company does not know which cars will be damaged, but they can anticipate a certain number based on the number of policyholders in the pool. The cost of auto insurance is based on a number of factors, including the age of the driver (sorry, but younger individuals have more accidents than people in their 40s), where the individual is located, the age and size of the vehicle, the cost to repair the vehicle, whether the individual is married, whether the state is a tort or no-fault state (Michigan is a no-fault state), and even the prevalence of bad weather (think Michigan winters . . .).

When you purchase an auto insurance policy (called a PAP), there are six primary sections that you as the insured should review to make sure everything is accurate. These include:

Part A: Liability

Part B: Medical Payments

Part C: Uninsured and under-insured motorist protection

Part D: Damage to your auto

Part E: Duties after an accident or loss

Part F: General provisions

Generally speaking, when you purchase insurance you will have PL/PD coverage of something like $50,000/$150,000/$50,000. The PL has to do with the first two numbers and refers to "Public Liability." In this example of 50/150, $50,000 would be the maximum limit on bodily injury for each person injured in an accident and $150,000 the maximum limit for bodily injury per accident. The PD refers to "Property Damage," and the $50,000 limit reflects the maximum coverage for damage to another's property. In Michigan, the state mandated limit for minimum PL/PD is 20/40/10. While everyone wants to pay the lowest possible amount for auto insurance, one really needs to be concerned about the coverage appropriate for the assets they have. For example, if you have assets of $500,000 and your liability overage covers only $50,000, if you are in an accident in which there is a $400,000 loss you may be required to pay the remaining $350,000 from your personal assets, if you go to court and a judgment is entered against you.

Life Insurance

Life insurance is one of those things most people do not like to talk about because it deals with their own mortality. It, however, needs to be considered in today's world as a critical part of any financial plan. There are a variety of life insurance products available today. I firmly believe that there are very few bad life insurance products; however, there is often bad application of the products. Life insurance policies generally fall into one of two categories: term and whole life. Term products are generally cheaper due to not having the buildup of cash values within the policy. Term life insurance is like homeowner's insurance; you will have life insurance protection as long as you continue to pay the premiums each year. The rates for the life insurance will vary based on the amounts of coverage you desire and the number of years you would like to be covered. At the end of this specified term, you have the option of renewing the policy (at higher rates) or letting it expire. One of the provisions you will want to have is guaranteed renewability, which will allow you to set up a new policy with the old provider even though you may not otherwise qualify because of heath-related issues.

Whole life insurance, and the host of variations on this type, boils down to having both term insurance and savings that build through cash value. As the cash value of such a policy increases, the insurance company's liability is reduced if something should happen to the insured person. For example, if a person has a $100,000 policy with a $50,000 cash value, the insurance company is responsible only for the additional $50,000 if a loss occurs. There is often a point at which the build-up of cash value will pay the costs of the life insurance protection. Although whole life is often recommended by agents—and scorned by the public press—it does provide life insurance protection for your entire life. The question is often asked whether you need life insurance for your entire life. If you follow the guidelines of this book, there should come a point at which you have set up accounts for college, paid off your home, and built up a savings surplus. At this point life insurance may become an unnecessary expense.

I am a firm believer that life insurance should be used to protect oneself against catastrophic events and not as an investment. Just as you should always have home owner's insurance if you own a home, life insurance is needed to protect your survivors should something detrimental happen to you. If you have small children and want to provide for their college education, provide spousal income for a number of years, and pay off your primary residence, purchase the amount of insurance you will need to accomplish this, and no more. Also, with the growing dependence on multiple household incomes, it may not be enough to cover just the primary breadwinner; both spouses may need insurance to cover, for example, the possible daycare needs should the spouse die unexpectedly.

Taxation

Benjamin Franklin once said that there are two certainties in life: death and taxes. Taxation is important to understand and needs to be a part of any comprehensive plan. Income can be broken down into three categories: wages/business income, investment income, and passive income. With each of these categories income must be reported on your annual tax return and is taxed based on the tax bracket you are in. When it comes to losses, you are limited to a certain amount each year, but it can be netted against any gains. With passive income, you can net against other passive income but cannot take an overall loss. When you add up these tax items you can derive your Adjusted Gross Income, which is what your state taxes are based on. When calculating your federal taxes, you would take the adjusted gross income, less personal exemptions for each person you are claiming, less the greater of the standard or itemized deduction. Of interesting note, tax policy changes often, and what is the case one year is often different the next.

In calculating taxes you can calculate your marginal and average tax bracket. Your marginal tax bracket is the percentage you would pay on the next dollar of income. The average rate is the amount of taxes you would pay overall, divided by your gross income. A common misconception is the idea that, as you move from one tax bracket to another, you will pay that rate on all of your income; this causes people to not want the income to move into that bracket. It is important to remember that you pay the higher tax rate only for the portion of income that would fall into the new bracket.

When it comes to taking the standard or itemized deduction, if you don't own a house you most likely will claim the standard deduction. This is what the IRS has determined to be the amount most people have in deductions. Only if your actual deductions are higher than the standard does it make sense to itemize.

Everyone likes to pay as little in taxes as possible. However, based on the electronic age the IRS is tracking more and more items that are reported on your tax return. Many people are afraid of the IRS because they often try to cheat. If you are honest, you really do not have much to worry about, especially with the low percentage of returns that are actually audited. Finally, if you have a right to a deduction and the IRS does not allow it, fight for it. There have been more than a few times over the past few years when I have fought for a deduction that was rightfully mine and won.

Retirement

Retirement is currently perceived as a period of time that is a reward for many years of working. Older current retirees have the benefits of a long life span, pensions, Social Security, and higher than average personal savings, as many of them learned the importance of personal savings going through the Depression.

Let's look at this in greater detail. When we talk about retirement we often talk about the three important legs of the retirement stool: personal savings, pensions, and Social Security. Many older retirees today experienced the effects of the Great Depression, which caused them to be one of the generations that saved the most. Many of these individuals lived in the Industrial Age, when pension programs were the norm, and many are currently receiving monthly benefit checks from their former employers. In addition, many of these individuals did not contribute greatly to Social Security based upon the year it was created and so are enjoying payments based on a long life expectancy.

When you consider all of these facts, you would expect the average older retiree to be very wealthy. In reality, however, only a small minority of current retirees earn more than $50,000 per year, with the majority earning less than $20,000 per year.

The changes in interest rates over the past few years have had a great effect upon current retirees. These changes benefit the people who have mortgages, but individuals on fixed incomes saw substantial reductions in their incomes as the interest rates fell.

These considerations, however, are nothing compared to the challenges the next generation of retirees will face!

Changes in Retirement Planning

One of the major challenges of retirement today is for the Baby Boomer population. The Baby Boomers were born between 1946 and 1964 and represent 78 million Americans, or 27.5

percent of the population of the United States. All of them are now over 50 years old, and many of them have not sufficiently planned for their retirement. Tomorrow's retirees will face a set of challenges including increased life spans, additional changes to Social Security benefits, changes in pension plans, and the lack of personal savings.

Although there has been some talk within the federal government regarding the problems the Social Security system will likely face, little is being done by Congress to address these potential challenges. In 2017 the Social Security Administration began paying more in benefits than was being collected through Social Security taxes, and by 2041 the Social Security Trust Fund is projected to be exhausted. At that point Social Security will be able to pay only 75 cents for each dollar of scheduled benefits.

Why is this not being addressed by today's politicians? Most of these changes are going to happen after the current politicians leave office. They are not worried about problems that may occur in the future and are concerned only about dealing with the backlash this issue will raise.

There are a number of questions that arise when you consider what Social Security does, and does not, cover. Social Security pays retirement, disability, family, and survivor benefits. In addition, various components of Social Security, such as Medicare, pay health expenses for inpatient hospital care, nursing care, doctors' fees, drugs, and other medical services and supplies for citizens 67 years of age and older, as well as for those who have been receiving disability benefits through Social Security.

When can you receive your benefits? Based on current Social Security regulations, if you were born before 1938 you could have retired with full benefits at age 65. In 1983 a change in the law caused the full retirement age to gradually increase to age 67 for people born after 1960. However, regardless of how old you are you can retire as early as age 62 and take benefits at a reduced rate. If you work beyond your full retirement age you can receive higher benefits based on additional earnings and credits.

As we look at the history of Social Security we will quickly realize that Social Security was never intended to be the sole provider of retirement income, nor was it intended to provide benefits for the life spans many are now enjoying. When Social Security was introduced, the average worker could be expected to retire at 62 and die at 67. The first recipients of Social Security benefits were typically on the program for only about 5 years. Compare that to today's retiree, who can retires as early as age 62 and be on Social Security for 25 years or longer.

A significant shift has also occurred in the retirement benefits offered by many major corporations. For many years the defined benefit plan, or pension, was the benefit of choice. At one time there were over 100,000 defined benefit plans. Today this number has dwindled to fewer than 30,000, as more and more companies are opting for the more contributory format that is used in many 401(k) plans.

There are a number of good reasons for this. For many years companies have assumed the investment risk when they guaranteed the benefits that were to be provided by the plan. This investment risk reduced the employer's earnings when markets were down, as the company was required to make up any amount in the event their plans were underfunded due to market decline; these contributions were taken directly from the earnings of the company.

Employees also liked the shift. Workers were changing employers more and more frequently and were often unable to earn a substantial benefit from these traditional pension plans. They are happier to have a more portable retirement plan that could be transferred from employer to employer. Since many of these participants were younger, they also believed that by investing their retirement funds in a more aggressive manner they could receive a higher level of return than what was available from their employer, thus providing a higher standard of living at retirement.

Another challenge is a lack of personal savings for the next generation of retirees. Most of the present and future Baby Boomer retirees have lived through a generation of excessive spending. By some accounts this generation spends more than has ever before been the case in the United States. An interesting fact is that, on average, a person has less than $2,500 in total personal savings today. When you ask people about their level of savings, most just pull out their wallet. This level of personal savings will not support an adequate level of retirement income.

When confronted by these facts, many Baby Boomers state that they will just have to work longer in the jobs they currently have. Unfortunately for them, this may not be an option. Due to the many changes that globalization and the digital age are bringing about, many of the current jobs may no longer exist in another 20 years, and these individuals may not have the necessary skills to compete on a global scale with younger, or possibly foreign, individuals for these positions.

The Goal of Becoming Debt Free

While this section may have fit better in the goals section of this book, I believe that the issue bears repeating here. The dream and goal of being debt free can be achieved! One of the goals of every individual or family reading this book should be to become debt free. Equipped with the necessary tools, becoming debt free can be achieved by anyone who will take the time to persevere toward this goal.

If you make this goal a priority, you will begin to look at some of your expenditures and choose whether to make a purchase for immediate gratification or to become debt free more quickly. Many individuals make other investments before they are debt free. Any investment has associated risks, and making investments too early may slow the process of becoming debt free.

In the next session we will be looking at these possible investments and their associated risks. Today, let's just make sure we have a good handle on the goals we would like to achieve in life. Take the time to make sure you've completed that earlier activity now before moving forward.

How Much Do I Need to Save?

According to Morningstar, 15% of your current salary should be saved each year as a minimum savings target. If you are a higher income earner, your figure may need to be even higher. However, it is important to remember that this figure includes both your investment and any match provided by your employer. In addition, Morningstar also provides some savings guidelines based on age to see whether you are on track with your saving. These guidelines suggest:

By age 35: 1x-2x your salary saved
By age 45: 3x-4x your salary saved
By age 55: 7x-8x your salary saved
By age 65: 10x-11x your salary saved

Various Types of Retirement Accounts

The government has done a good job of offering a number of options from which you can select as you save for your retirement. This section will not only present the available options but also explain the tax effects of these types of accounts, to allow you to maximize your long-term returns.

Reviewing the Tax Effect

One of the questions that often arises concerning retirement investments is this: Should I pay the tax now, or should I contribute toward my retirement on a pre-tax basis and allow the investments to grow tax deferred until the funds are withdrawn?. The question is not *whether* but *when* we will pay the taxes.

The question of paying taxes now or later comes down to this: Do you think tax rates will be lower now or in the future? Many people believe that their incomes will be much lower in retirement and that it will therefore be beneficial for them to wait and pay these taxes when the funds are withdrawn later in life There may be many instances in which the government will need additional income in the future to fund all of the benefits it has promised the American people. Income levels may go down in retirement, but tax rates may significantly increase. Therefore, it may be wise to use Roth type strategies that require the payment of taxes today but impose no income taxes when the funds are eventually withdrawn.

Defined Contribution vs. Defined Benefit Accounts

When you plan your retirement and the various accounts available to you, you also need to consider retirement plans offered by your employer. Employer retirement plans fall into two major categories: defined contribution and defined benefit. Traditionally throughout the Industrial Age many companies provided a pension, which was part of a defined benefit plan. A defined benefit plan specifies the amount you will receive each month based on a number of factors, such as years of service with your employer. Defined benefit plans provide you this benefit without any investment risk, as all of the risk is borne by the employer. Employees are required to contribute annually to these plans during their working years, based on the amount calculated to be held in order to provide the promised benefits.

As we move from the Industrial Age, more and more companies are shifting from defined benefit plans to defined contribution plans. There is no specified benefit with these plans; benefits are based on the match or profit sharing contributions of the employer, the amount deferred by the employee, and the performance of the investments the employee selects. This type of plan tends to be more attractive to younger employees, who are able to invest their funds at higher levels of risk in the hope of achieving a higher level of return. All investment risk is shifted from the employer to the employee. This is beneficial to the employer, who doesn't need to contribute greater amounts, thus reducing company profits, during times of overall market decline.

Both of these types of plans offer various benefits to the employee. It would not be fair to say that one is better than the other; they just operate differently. A discussion of the various forms of these plans follow.

Pensions

A pension plan is part of the defined benefit family of retirement plans. A pension is an amount paid to a former employee as a benefit for the years of service she has given to the employer. For example, if someone gives 40 years of service to the employer, the employer will provide a fixed benefit each month for as long as the employee lives. This amount will vary based on the provisions of the plan but generally will include either a fixed component, such as an amount per year times the number of years the employee worked for the company, or a percentage benefit based on the salary of the employee over the last years of work. Pensions are of great benefit to most people and are often a substantial part of their retirement income.

Due to the recent variation in the overall financial markets, these types of plans, which historically have been associated with a unionized environment, are being phased out with preference given to the more popular, but less predictable, defined contribution plans such as 401(k)s in order to not become a financial burden on an employer during times of poor market returns.

401(k)

A 401k is a defined contribution plan that relates to a section in the IRS tax code that permits employees to tax defer current income until retirement. It allows an employer to provide an incentive to employees through a potential employer match and also allows for the benefits of profit sharing. The amount the employee can contribute to the plan each year varies based on IRS cost-of-living guidelines; it is, however, rather substantial and is of significant benefit to employees. In addition, those employees who are older than 50 years of age can contribute additional amounts as a "catch-up" contribution.

> **PRACTICAL EXAMPLE**
>
> *ABC Company offers a 401k with a match of 50% of the first six percent. If an employee were to contribute 4%, the employer would also contribute for the employee's benefit half of this amount or 2%. If the employee contributes 6%, the employer would match by 3%. If the employee contributes 10% of his salary, the employer would again contribute the 3%. In this scenario it would be most beneficial to the employee to contribute at least 6% in order to maximize the employer match.*

Many of the 401k plans, although they have similar provisions, as required by a number of governmental agencies such as the Internal Revenue Service or a governmental act called the Employee Retirement Income Security Act (ERISA), offer various options based on the goals and objectives of the employer. It is very important that each person who contributes to this type of plan obtains and reads a summary plan description, which highlights the plan's provisions and benefits to the employee.

Typically, a 401(k) account offers a number of mutual funds or even company stock as potential investment options. Most plans require at least three investment options (money market, bond fund, and stock fund), but many provide more, sometimes even numbering into the hundreds. It is important to consider the quality of the funds or family of funds, as well as the associated fees charged when looking at these options. Often companies that are looking to minimize their administrative fees offer plans that charge higher asset fees, which increases the expense to the employee and lowers the performance of the funds.

It is important to remember that all contributions to a normal 401k account, though tax-deferred, require payment of the tax when the proceeds are withdrawn. A new wrinkle in the 401k market is to offer Roth-like 401(k)s that require the employee to pay tax on current contributions but do not require any payment of tax when the funds are withdrawn at retirement. An additional provision that is expected to be added to these plans is automatic enrollment, whereby the employee is automatically enrolled, at a minimal amount, upon eligibility and can opt out only by declining the plan.

IRA

An Individual Retirement Account or IRA is a form of tax-deferred account that is used to fund part of an individual's retirement.

Persons who are younger than 70½ and have earned income are eligible to participate in an IRA. In the traditional form, individuals can contribute to these accounts, take a tax reduction on these contributions, and allow these contributed amounts to grow tax-free until they are withdrawn. When the funds are withdrawn after age 59½, the amounts withdrawn are subject to ordinary income taxes. If the individual still has any money in these accounts after age 70½, there are minimum amounts that must be withdrawn each year. If the funds are withdrawn before age 59½ there is usually a 10% penalty in addition to the normal tax on these withdrawals. In addition, if an individual has another retirement account provided by his employer, he will be able to put additional amounts into an IRA account. Unfortunately, many people do not understand these accounts. According to the Investment Company Institute, only 14 percent of Americans make annual contributions to an IRA.

A variation of the traditional IRA is the Roth IRA. With a Roth IRA you receive no current tax benefit for contributions made to this account, but there will be no taxes due when the funds are withdrawn in the future. With this type of account there is no minimum withdrawal at age 70½, and you can contribute to it even after this age. Whether you select a Roth or the traditional type or IRA depends again on your view of what will happen to tax rates in the future, especially if they go up, as predicted. If you are younger, this type of account could provide significant benefits over the traditional type if you hold it for many years.

One option few people know about is their ability to transfer a traditional IRA into a Roth IRA. If you have earned income of less than a certain amount (currently $100,000), you can convert your traditional IRAs into Roth IRAs and pay the income tax on the amounts converted now instead of in the future. Although this may not seem like a good tax strategy, paying income on these amounts now, while the overall tax rates are lower, will cause any future earnings to be tax free and permit one to avoid potentially higher future taxes.

> **PRACTICAL EXAMPLE**
>
> *Bill and Mary have a $5 million-dollar estate and a $75,000 annual income. $1 million dollars of this estate is in traditional IRA accounts. As they would like to minimize their eventual estate taxes, Bill and Mary can convert these IRA accounts into a Roth account to reduce the actual size of their estate and avoid estate taxes on these distributions.*

Both of these plans are good for investors for saving for retirement. However, based on a number of governmental indicators I am not sure the government will be able to maintain the Roth accounts indefinitely. The government may either suspend future contributions or eliminate these accounts entirely in order to gain the tax benefits of these accounts.

SIMPLE Plan

Savings Incentive Match Plan for Employees of Small Employers (SIMPLE) plans are available to companies with fewer than 100 employees. This popular plan offers a number of benefits to both the employee and the employer. For the employee it allows tax-deferment of the contributions until retirement. For the employer it is a very cost-effective plan to start and manage. The employee benefits from this plan because the employer is required to either match the first 3% of the employee's contribution for those employees who participate or to match the first 2% of all of the employees' income regardless of whether they contribute to the plan. These types of plans can be set up as a 401(k), but most use the simpler method and use an IRA account. Inasmuch as these accounts are in effect IRAs, the IRA rules for distributions also apply to the SIMPLE accounts.

403(b) Plans

A 403(b) plan is like a 401(k) in that it is based on a provision in the tax code and authorizes tax deferral contributions for nonprofit organizations. This plan is similar to the 401(k) in that it permits the same tax deferral of employee contributions and provides for an employer match. The plan can be set up as an employee sponsored plan, in which the employee can work with a number of approved investment providers, or an employer sponsored plan, in which there is one company with which the employer contracts to provide this service. One of the major differences in the 403(b) plan is the additional "catch-up" provisions for those who have longer periods of service on top of the provisions that are normally available for those over 50 years of age. If you would like to learn more about these types of plans and their benefits, you can download Publication 571 from the IRS website.

457 Plans

457 plans are nonqualified tax advantaged plans for government employees. For example, as a state school, Grand Valley State University in Western Michigan offers this type of plan to all of its employees. The limits for a 457 plan are normally identical to those of the 403(b) and 401(k) plans.

Special Accounts for Business Owners

There are several accounts that can be set up for small business owners that will provide a number of retirement benefits. One of the more popular accounts for the single business owner is the Simplified Employee Pension (SEP) or the newer Solo 401(k). The SEP allows you to contribute a portion of your earnings to an IRA account at a rate that is higher than that of a normal IRA contribution. It is interesting that with this type of plan one can still contribute to the IRA, in addition to the SEP account. With a Solo 401(k) you must not have any employees (with the exception of your spouse); the plan allows contributions of up to 100% of your income. There is significant cost savings with each of these plans over those of the more traditional plans. Many of them cost just $10 per year for administration.

Estate Planning

Inheritances

Inheritances are one of those life areas that become very personal in nature and about which there is little definite agreement. For some, the leaving of funds to children is a normal part of generational aging. Others would rather give their life savings to anyone else before passing down any money to their children. In one case I know of a wealthy businessman who set up each of his children financially while he was alive, allowing him to see the fruits of these investments in his children. However, all future funds will be going to charity.

While we may not all agree on the best methods for passing down these funds, I believe that this conversation is necessary, as over the next few years trillions will be passed down from the current older retirees to the Baby Boomers. While we have already stated that the current older retirees are the most saving generation and that the Baby Boomers are those who spend the most, the facts are that these funds will be transferred down to the next generation unless we create legal agreements to the contrary.

The decision to include one's children or to donate one's inheritance to charities or other organizations becomes a personal one for which we must all plan. The bottom line is that you came into this world with nothing and are going to leave with nothing. Everything you have will be distributed to others. At that point the only remaining questions will *to whom* and *how much*? By taking the time to plan ahead for our estates through wills and trusts, we can at least know that our estate will go to the individuals and organizations we decide they should go to.

If you are concerned about how your children will deal with the proceeds from your estate, there is an old but relevant quote that says "Do your giving while you are living so you are knowing where it is going." For some that may be difficult, as they might not know how much they may need for the rest of their life. However, if we start our giving earlier in life—even small amounts of money—we can observe the recipients handling the money, see them enjoy it, and further teach them how to handle the inheritance they will receive later in their life.

The Reality of the Future

Benjamin Franklin once stated that there are only two certainties in life: death and taxes. While we do not like to talk about the future and our ultimate death, the realities are that we will all at one point pass on and must prepare our finances for that day. In reality today, there are many who work their entire lives making money, only to lose it all through the probate process.

In the Beginning There Is the Will

One of the most basic but important estate documents is the will. The will provides a number of things, including naming the people to handle your estate when you die and specifying who will receive particular items of your property, how other items of your property should be distributed, and who should take care of any minor children. While the first two benefits of a will may not be that important, the naming of a guardian for your children may be one of the most important benefits of having a will. While you may have limited assets and feel a will to be unnecessary, the naming of a guardian is very important; if you do not specify one the courts will step in and do so for you. In my case, the guardians my wife and I named for our children would probably not have been the ones named by the court. Bottom line: Whom would you prefer to have name this guardian, you or the courts? Oftentimes people do not like to think about creating a will because it forces them to recognize that they are not immortal and will someday in the future leave this earth.

Health Care Power of Attorney

Many of you remember the issues surrounding Terry Schiavo and the court case in Florida surrounding her wishes and her ultimate death. One of the primary reasons her life was played out on a national stage was her not having drafted a health care power of attorney. The health care power of attorney is a relatively simple document that is often overlooked when preparing for one's estate. The health care power of attorney basically provides two important things. First, it names the person you would like to have make your health care decisions for you when you cannot make them yourself. This could be a primary person, such as your spouse, or a contingent beneficiary, in the event the primary person might not be able to serve. Second, it specifies your wishes should you become incapacitated. The normal choice for a person in a vegetative state to keep them alive if at all possible, even if that means doing so by machine; to maintain their status unless there is very little change; or to have the plug pulled, allowing them to die. When you make these decisions in advance for yourself or write out these statements, it is important to make sure you are incorporating the specific language your states requires. This is one of the reasons you need to solicit the services of an attorney as you prepare these documents.

Trusts

Trusts are an often misunderstood part of estate planning. While this section will not be from a legal perspective, it will provide some basic facts that can be helpful to you in deciding whether you need to have a trust document written for you. A trust is a separate estate-planning document that does not replace any of the other documents. A trust is a legal document that will determine how your estate should be settled, the people involved in that settlement, where and who should receive your money, and when they should receive the money and other properties. For some of you who are reading this, it may sound as though the trust duplicates some of the functions of the will, which is a partially correct observation. If you have a trust, you would also have a very simple will specifying that all of the assets you may have forgotten to mention in the trust be included in it. The major advantage of a trust is that it avoids the costs and time of probate, and if you have significant assets it can allow you to double your allowable exclusion for estate tax purposes. To determine whether a trust would be an advantage to you, it is important to consider three areas: the assets that would go through probate, the size of your estate, and your family structure. In many cases individuals hold assets that would not go through probate, including assets held in retirement or IRA accounts, insurance or annuity products, or assets that are held under joint names. In all of these cases the assets would transfer outside of probate to the beneficiaries or to the other joint owners. If all of your assets would bypass probate already, you would not need to create a trust to accomplish this.

The second determining factor is the size of your estate. If you have a sizeable estate of more than a million dollars, a trust may provide you some significant tax advantages. Everyone is currently allowed to transfer certain amounts of money from one generation to another without paying any taxes on that transfer. However, the tax laws are constantly changing, as is the amount that is excluded from taxation; if you have amounts that go above the current limits the tax rates charged can be very steep. For some it may seem as though they have worked their entire lives to get ahead, only to lose half in taxes when they die. By using separate trusts you and your spouse can each take advantage of the available estate tax exclusion and save a considerable amount of tax. However, if your assets are less than a million, the tax benefits may not warrant the creation and costs of creating a trust.

The third area to consider is your particular family structure. Let me give you an example of a possible estate situation. Let's say you have a mixed marriage, with each of you having three children (just think of the old television show *The Brady Bunch*). Let's say that the majority of the assets in the marriage came from the wife as a life insurance settlement from her former husband. One day the couple was involved in a car accident, and the wife was killed instantly, but the husband lived for 30 days before he died. In this case, depending on how their will was written, all of the assets of the wife could be given to the husband upon her death, and transferred upon his death to his children, completely eliminating all benefits for the children of the wife. While this may be an extreme example, it could happen. If you have a mixed marriage and want to ensure that all of the assets go back to your children, a trust may make sense just to protect the assets. While there are a number of other considerations, if you do not have very many assets and do not have a mixed marriage, if may be more cost effective to create a will instead of the trust.

If you do create a trust, one important reminder is to retitle your assets or to "fund" your trust. If you simply create the trust document and do nothing with the assets of your estate, the effectiveness of the trust will be lost.

Do We Need an Attorney to Help Us in the Estate Process?

There are a number of ways in which a will can be created, including handwriting it (often called a holographic will), using a template that can be obtained on the internet or through software programs or books, or hiring the services of an attorney. While an attorney can be costly, there is often a significant benefit for using one. One important consideration in selecting whether to use an attorney comes down to a specific point. When creating other legal documents, if something is not created properly it can oftentimes be revised to fix the issues. However, if there are problems with a will, or if the the document you produced proves to be invalid, the only time this would likely be discovered is after you had expired—when you unfortunately could no longer change the document. There is also a certain amount of state-related terminology that must be included in the document in order for the will to be valid within the state you reside in. While I often suggest that you avoid spending money, this is one area in which it is important to spend some money. It often does not cost any more to hire an estate planning attorney who is a specialist in this area rather than simply choosing an attorney you might normally use for commercial documents or corporate actions. An estate planning attorney focuses on wills and trusts and is an expert in this area. As tax laws and legislation change frequently, it is important to find a person who keeps up with all of these changes and can become creative with regard to how the estate is handled.

Attorneys often charge by the hour, so it is important to establish up front how you wish to have the estate handled. Here are some questions that should be answered before going to an attorney:

- Are there any personal items you would like to have go to specific individuals?
- Whom do you want to appoint to take care of your affairs after you die? Who would be the contingent person in case this individual might be unavailable or unwilling to serve?
- Whom would you want to appoint to take care of your minor children if you were to die or become incapacitated? If they are unavailable or unwilling, whom would you select as a contingent care provider?
- What powers do you want to give your personal representative?

As you review these items, there needs to be a comprehensive list developed for each question asked. Often, named individuals have died already or are unable to perform the services that you request. I have known some cases in which the couple had divorced and family members of the divorced spouses were named, causing significant relational problems as the estate and guardianship were settled.

Putting Together the Comprehensive Plan

While we have had a quick journey together, it is now time to put together the entire plan. This plan will include the financial statements we created in the first session, the goals we have established for the next few years, and the budgets we created to not only pay for our day-to-day expenses but to fund our longer-term goals. The plan also looks at the benefits provided by our employers and whatever other benefits we need to supplement these. This would include additional amounts in retirement accounts. In addition, what investments would be appropriate for us? Finally, we need to create an estate plan. I think you will agree that financial planning and investing is not one-dimensional but considers many different factors. I hope you have enjoyed this process and have learned about yourself through it.

It is my hope that through effective planning all your goals will become realities!

Worksheet 1: Debt Listing Worksheet

Outstanding Bills	Rate	Current Balance
Credit Card 1		
Credit Card 2		
Auto 1		
Auto 2		
Home Mortgage		
Second Mortgage		
Student Debt		
Other		
Other		
Other		
Other		
Other		
Other		
Other		
Other		
	Total Debts:	

Worksheet 2: Balance Sheet

Assets (Things That You Own)

Item	Current value:
Checking Accounts	_____
Savings Accounts	_____
Investment Accounts	_____
Retirement Accounts	_____
Cash Value of Life Insurance	_____
Home	_____
Autos	_____
Jewelry	_____
Other _____	_____
Other _____	_____
Total Household Assets:	_____

Debts (Amounts That You Owe)

Total from Debt Listing Worksheet   _____

Net Worth: _____

Note: Take the total assets and subtract total debts to arrive at your net worth.

Worksheet 3: A Successful Life

If you were to look back on your life from your deathbed, what would you want to have accomplished to say that your life had been successful?

_____
_____
_____
_____
_____
_____
_____
_____
_____
_____
_____
_____
_____
_____
_____
_____
_____
_____
_____
_____
_____
_____
_____

Worksheet 4: Long-Term Goals

Worksheet 5: 5-Year Prioritized Goals

Goal Area   **Specific Goal**

Worksheet 6: Goal Development Form

Priority   **Goal Area**   **Specific Goal**

_____   _____   _____

Potential Obstacles to Achieving Goal: _____
Goal Timetable: _____
Accountability Person: _____
Action Steps
1) _____
2) _____
3) _____

Priority   **Goal Area**   **Specific Goal**

_____   _____   _____

Potential Obstacles to Achieving Goal: _____
Goal Timetable: _____
Accountability Person: _____
Action Steps
1) _____
2) _____
3) _____

Priority   **Goal Area**   **Specific Goal**

_____   _____   _____

Potential Obstacles to Achieving Goal: _____
Goal Timetable: _____
Accountability Person: _____
Action Steps
1) _____
2) _____
3) _____

Priority   **Goal Area**   **Specific Goal**

_____   _____   _____

Potential Obstacles to Achieving Goal: _____

Goal Timetable: _____

Accountability Person: _____

Action Steps

1) _____
2) _____
3) _____

Priority   **Goal Area**   **Specific Goal**

_____   _____   _____

Potential Obstacles to Achieving Goal: _____

Goal Timetable: _____

Accountability Person: _____

Action Steps

1) _____
2) _____
3) _____

Priority   **Goal Area**   **Specific Goal**

_____   _____   _____

Potential Obstacles to Achieving Goal: _____

Goal Timetable: _____

Accountability Person: _____

Action Steps

1) _____
2) _____
3) _____

Worksheet 7: Variable Expenses

Periodic Income Payments

	Annual Amount	Monthly Amount
Bonuses – Primary	_____	_____
Bonuses – Secondary	_____	_____
Income Tax Refunds	_____	_____
Other _____	_____	_____
Other _____	_____	_____
Total Monthly Amount:		_____

Periodic Expense Payments

	Annual Amount	Monthly Amount
Insurances: Auto	_____	_____
Medical: Doctors	_____	_____
Medical: Dentists	_____	_____
Birthday Presents	_____	_____
Christmas Presents	_____	_____
Property Taxes	_____	_____
Children's School Expenses	_____	_____
Vacations	_____	_____
Other _____	_____	_____
Other _____	_____	_____
Other _____	_____	_____
Total Monthly Amount:		_____

Worksheet 8: First-Pass Budget

Monthly Income

Primary _____

Secondary _____

Other Income _____

Total Monthly Income _____

Monthly Expenses

Taxes (Fed/State/FICA) _____

Housing _____

Communications (Tele/Internet/Cell) _____

Utilities _____

Home: Maintenance/Fees _____

Housing: Other Expenses _____

Giving to Others (Charitable Giving) _____

Food _____

Insurances _____

Auto(s) _____

Debt/Credit Card Payments _____

Hobbies _____

Entertainment _____

Vacations _____

Children/Childcare _____

Medical _____

Clothing   _____

Savings   _____

Miscellaneous Expenses   _____

Monthly Variable Expenses (Worksheet 1)   _____

                 Total Monthly Expenses: _____

                     The Bottom Line (+/-): _____

         (Monthly Income Minus Expenses)

Worksheet 9: Suggested Budget Spending Ranges

Monthly Income

Primary	_____
Secondary	_____
Other Income	_____
Total Monthly Income	100%

Monthly Expenses

Taxes (Fed/State/FICA)	19.9% (taken out before the other expenses)
Housing	32%
Communications (Tele/Internet/Cell)	(included in housing)
Utilities	(included in housing)
Home: Maintenance/Fees	(included in housing)
Housing: Other Expenses	(included in housing)
Giving to Others (Charitable Giving)	(included in housing)
Food	12%
Insurances	5%
Auto(s)	14%
Debt/Credit Card Payments	5%
Hobbies	(included in entertainment)
Entertainment	7%
Vacations	(included in entertainment)
Children/Childcare	5%
Medical	4%
Clothing	6%
Savings	5%
Miscellaneous Expenses	5%

    Monthly Variable Expenses (Worksheet 1) _____

        Total Monthly Expenses: _____

        The Bottom Line (+/-): _____

    (Monthly Income Minus Expenses)

Worksheet 10: Budget Comparison to Ranges

Monthly Income	Current	Percentage	Recommend
Primary	_____	_____	_____
Secondary	_____	_____	_____
Other Income	_____	_____	_____
Total Monthly Income	100%	100%	100%

Monthly Expenses			
Taxes (Fed/State/FICA)	_____	_____	_____
Housing	_____	_____	_____
Communications (Tele/Internet/Cell)	_____	_____	_____
Utilities	_____	_____	_____
Home: Maintenance/Fees	_____	_____	_____
Housing: Other Expenses	_____	_____	_____
Giving to Others (Charitable Giving)	_____	_____	_____
Food	_____	_____	_____
Insurances	_____	_____	_____
Auto(s)	_____	_____	_____
Debt/Credit Card Payments	_____	_____	_____
Hobbies	_____	_____	_____
Entertainment	_____	_____	_____
Vacations	_____	_____	_____
Children/Childcare	_____	_____	_____

Medical	_____	_____	_____
Clothing	_____	_____	_____
Savings	_____	_____	_____
Miscellaneous Expenses	_____	_____	_____
Monthly Variable Expenses (Worksheet 1)	_____	_____	_____
Total Monthly Expenses:	_____	_____	_____
The Bottom Line (+/-):	_____	_____	_____

(Monthly Income Minus Expenses)

Worksheet 11: Absolutes/Non-Absolutes

**Single Person/Spouse
1 Absolutes**

_____
_____
_____
_____
_____
_____
_____
_____
_____

**Spouse
2 Absolutes**

_____
_____
_____
_____
_____
_____
_____
_____
_____

**Single Person/Spouse
1 Non-Absolutes**

_____
_____
_____
_____
_____
_____
_____
_____
_____

**Spouse
2 Non-Absolutes**

_____
_____
_____
_____
_____
_____
_____
_____
_____

Worksheet 12: Goal Costs

Goal	Cost of Goal	Monthly Savings Required
Retirement	_____	_____
_____	_____	_____
_____	_____	_____
_____	_____	_____
_____	_____	_____
_____	_____	_____
_____	_____	_____
_____	_____	_____
_____	_____	_____
_____	_____	_____
_____	_____	_____
_____	_____	_____
_____	_____	_____
_____	_____	_____
_____	_____	_____
_____	_____	_____
_____	_____	_____
_____	_____	_____
_____	_____	_____
_____	_____	_____
_____	_____	_____

Worksheet 13: Debt Snowball

Outstanding Bill	**Rate**	**Current Balance**
_____	_____	_____
_____	_____	_____
_____	_____	_____
_____	_____	_____
_____	_____	_____
_____	_____	_____
_____	_____	_____
_____	_____	_____
_____	_____	_____
_____	_____	_____
_____	_____	_____
_____	_____	_____
_____	_____	_____
_____	_____	_____
_____	_____	_____
_____	_____	_____
_____	_____	_____
_____	_____	_____
_____	_____	_____
_____	_____	_____

Total Monthly Payment: _____

Worksheet 14: Ideas for Balancing the Budget

Expense Item	Action That Can Be Taken	Potential Monthly Savings
_____	_____	_____
_____	_____	_____
_____	_____	_____
_____	_____	_____
_____	_____	_____
_____	_____	_____
_____	_____	_____
_____	_____	_____
_____	_____	_____
_____	_____	_____
_____	_____	_____
_____	_____	_____
_____	_____	_____
_____	_____	_____
_____	_____	_____
_____	_____	_____
_____	_____	_____
_____	_____	_____
_____	_____	_____

Total Monthly Payment: _____

Worksheet 15: Revised Final Budget

Monthly Income	Original	Revised
Primary	_____	_____
Secondary	_____	_____
Other Income	_____	_____
Total Monthly Income	_____	_____
Monthly Expenses		
Taxes (Fed/State/FICA)	_____	_____
Housing	_____	_____
Communications (Tele/Internet/Cell)	_____	_____
Utilities	_____	_____
Home: Maintenance/Fees	_____	_____
Housing: Other Expenses	_____	_____
Giving to Others (Charitable Giving)	_____	_____
Food	_____	_____
Insurances	_____	_____
Auto(s)	_____	_____
Debt/Credit Card Payments	_____	_____
Hobbies	_____	_____
Entertainment	_____	_____
Vacations	_____	_____
Children/Childcare	_____	_____
Medical	_____	_____
Clothing	_____	_____

Savings _____ _____

Miscellaneous Expenses _____ _____

Monthly Variable Expenses
(Worksheet 1) _____ _____

Total Monthly Expenses: _____ _____

The Bottom Line (+/-): _____ _____

(Monthly Income Minus Expenses)

Worksheet 16: Employer Benefits Checklist

Coverage Area	Provider/Coverage	Monthly Payment Required
Healthcare	_____	_____
Dental	_____	_____
Vision	_____	_____
Short-Term Disability	_____	_____
Long-Term Disability	_____	_____
Life Insurance	_____	_____

Other Benefits

_____   _____
_____   _____
_____   _____
_____   _____
_____   _____
_____   _____
_____   _____
_____   _____
_____   _____
_____   _____

Worksheet 17: Savings Plan

Taxable

Category	Security	Amount per Month	Target
Cash	Checking Account	_____	_____
Cash	Emergency Fund	_____	_____
_____	_____	_____	_____
_____	_____	_____	_____
_____	_____	_____	_____
_____	_____	_____	_____
_____	_____	_____	_____
_____	_____	_____	_____
_____	_____	_____	_____

Tax Advantaged

_____	_____	_____	_____
_____	_____	_____	_____
_____	_____	_____	_____
_____	_____	_____	_____
_____	_____	_____	_____

Worksheet 18: Insurance Needs

Coverage Area	Coverage	Monthly Payment Required
Auto	_____	_____
Auto	_____	_____
Home	_____	_____
Life Insurance	_____	_____
Umbrella	_____	_____

Other Insurance	Coverage	Monthly Payment Required
	_____	_____
	_____	_____
	_____	_____
	_____	_____
	_____	_____
	_____	_____
	_____	_____

Worksheet 19: Estate Planning Document

Testator: _____

Executor: _____

_____ (Secondary)

Beneficiaries

_____

_____

_____

Specific Items

_____

_____

_____

Children: _____

_____ (Secondary)

Healthcare POA: _____

_____ (Secondary)

Durable POA: _____

_____ (Secondary)

NOTES

NOTES